THE COSTUMEMAKER'S ART

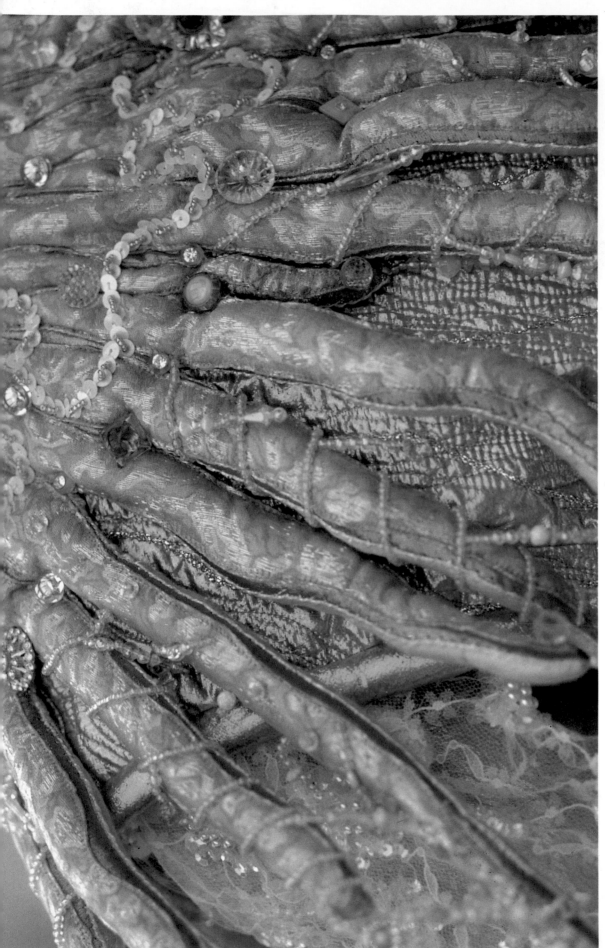

Published in 1992 by Lark Books
50 College Street
Asheville, North Carolina,
   U.S.A., 28801

Copyright © 1992, Lark Books

Editor: Thom Boswell
Design: Thom Boswell
   & Marcia Winters
Layout & Production:
   Thom Boswell
Typesetting: Elaine Thompson

ISBN 0-937274-58-5

Library of Congress Cataloging-in-
Publication Data
The Costumemaker's Art : cloaks
   of fantasy, masks of revelation /
   edited by Thom Boswell
         p.   cm.
   Includes index.
   ISBN 0-937274-58-5
   1. Wearable art–United States–
Themes, motives.   2. Costume–
United States–History–20th century–
Themes, motives
I. Boswell, Thom.   II. Lark Books
NK4860.5.U6C6 1992
746.9'2'0973–dc20   90-63600
                           CIP

All rights reserved.

All costume artists and photog-
raphers represented in this book
maintain full copyrights to their
work.

Every effort has been made to
ensure that all information in this
book is accurate. However, due
to differing conditions, tools, and
individual skills, the publisher cannot be responsible for any injuries,
losses, or other damages which
may result from the use of
the information in this book.

Printed in Hong Kong.

**Detail of "The Chrystal Maiden from
the Isle of Fire and Ice" (left). Design &
Construction: Christen Brown & Carol
McKie Manning; Model: Jean Olson;
Photo: Tom Henderson.**

**"When the Medicine Woman Weaves
her Spell, the Snake Charmer Begins
to Dance" (opposite). Credits: same
as above.**

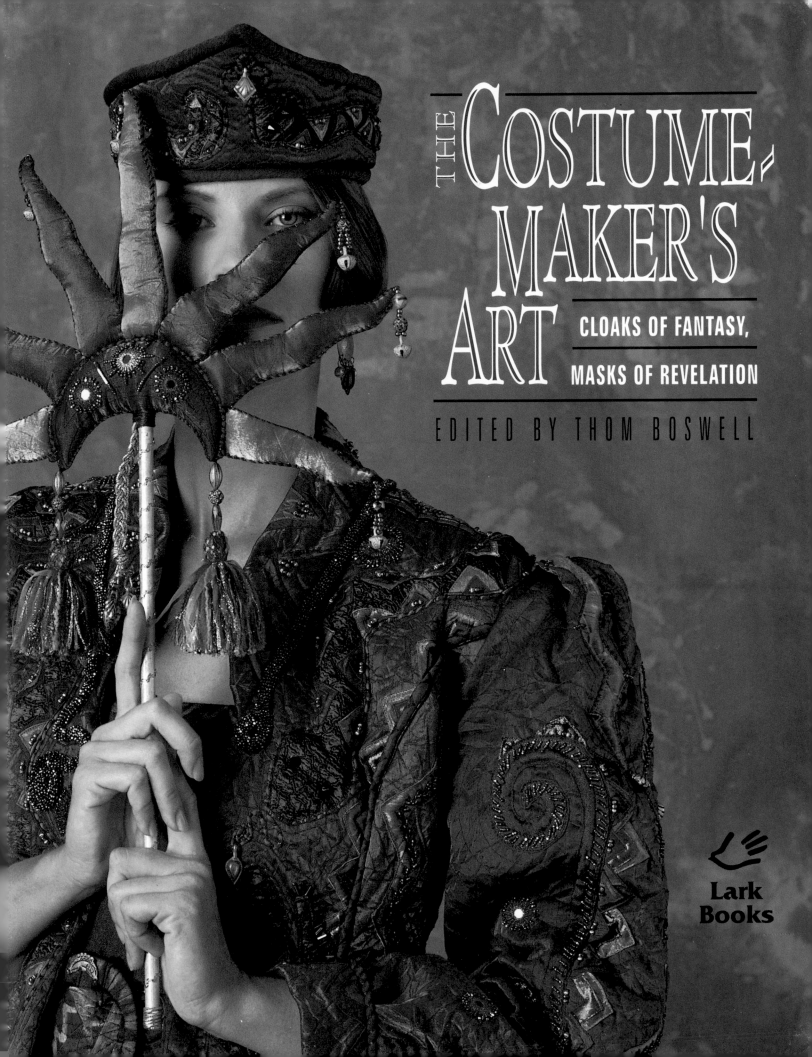

THE COSTUME-MAKER'S ART

CLOAKS OF FANTASY, MASKS OF REVELATION

EDITED BY THOM BOSWELL

Lark Books

TABLE OF CONTENTS

Preface **6**

The New Art of Costume **8**

The Essence of Costumemaking **13**

HISTORIC

VICTORIA RIDENOUR &
   ADRIAN BUTTERFIELD **18**
JANET WILSON ANDERSON **21**
LITA SMITH-GHARET **22**
KENNETH ALLEN **23**
BARB SCHOFIELD **24**
THE SOFT TOUCH **26**
JWLHYFER DE WINTER **28**
LANI TUCKER **30**
PATRICIA RICKARD **31**
JANA KEELER **32**
CHERIE MOORE **33**
ANIMAL X **34**
ANGELIQUE TROUVERE **35**
JENNIFER TIFFT **36**
JEANNETTE HOLLOMAN **36**
HISTORICAL REENACTMENT **37**
ELIZABETH PIDGEON &
   CARL ONTIS **38**
CAROLYN SALEMI **40**
JEANNIE TRIMMER **41**
MELA HOYT-HEYDON & FRIENDS **41**

FANTASTIC

ANIMAL X **42**
JULIA ANN HYLL **46**
VANDY VANDERVORT **48**
ROBIN LEWIS **50**
DENICE GIRARDEAU **52**
SALLY FINK **53**
KAREN KUYKENDALL **54**
DANA & BRUCE MACDERMOTT **56**
OFF THE WALL **58**
CAROLYN SALEMI **60**
RAE BRADBURY **61**
JANET WILSON ANDERSON **62**
WENDY ROSS **64**
JENNIFER KETCHAM **67**
VICTORIA RIDENOUR &
   ADRIAN BUTTERFIELD **68**
KARL HOPF **70**
DIANE KOVALCIN **70**
JOHN PETERS **71**
DENNIS MILLER **71**
PATRICIA BLACK **72**
PHIL GILLIAM **74**
ANYA MARTIN **74**
FIONA LEONARD **75**
KATHRYN MAYER **76**
KAREN & RICKY DICK **78**
ELIZABETH MAYBERRY & FRIENDS **82**
PATRICIA HAMMER **84**
LAUREL CUNNINGHAM-HILL **84**
SUSAN & JEFF STRINGER **85**
MARIAN & STEPHEN
   O'BRIEN-CLARK **86**
SELINA & MARK HARJU **87**
BARB SCHOFIELD **88**
MEG HIGGINS **90**
SUSAN TAUBENECK & FRIENDS **90**
SHELLY GOTTSCHAMER **91**
JULIE ZETTERBERG **92**
DEBORAH STRUB **93**
SANDY & PIERRE PETTINGER **94**
DEBORAH JONES **96**
ELEANOR FARRELL **98**
ANGELIQUE TROUVERE **100**
KATHY & DREW SANDERS **102**
JENNIFER TIFFT **106**
KEVIN ROCHE **108**
CYNTHIA FENA **110**
JULIE NICKELL **110**
MARJII ELLERS **111**
JACQUELINE WARD **112**
SHA SHA HIGBY **116**

FUTURISTIC

ESTELLE AKAMINE **122**
JANUWA MOJA **127**
TERRY NIEDZIALEK **128**
CHRISTEN BROWN &
   CAROL MCKIE MANNING **130**
SUSAN NININGER **132**
ZEPHRA MAY MILLER **136**
RENEE SHERRER **137**
MARILYN ANNIN **138**
JUNG HAE KIM **142**

Costumers' Guilds **144**

Index **144**

"Through a Gold Window" (opposite), a sculptural performance work. Design, Construction & Model: Sha Sha Higby; Photo: Richard Connelly.

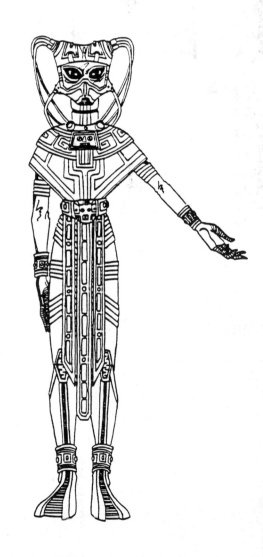

Drawing of "Croïian in Atmosphere Control Suit," by Alison Dayne Frankel.

Preface

Ever since Adam's fig leaf, humans have fabricated their own clothing and self-adornment. The dual concerns of function and beauty have always influenced the finished product, but in the case of costuming: aesthetics reign supreme.

Human artifice is perhaps most pronounced and pervasive as it celebrates its own form—the human body—in its many personae. Indeed, while "artifice" is a contrivance of human artfulness, as opposed to a product of Nature, it is a profoundly *natural* expression of human experience, and therefore not the least bit "artificial" or unnatural in the mundane sense.

The art of costuming has been practiced and developed since the beginnings of human culture—not only to enhance our everyday garments, but for a variety of other functions. Through symbolic ornamentation, designations of rank and office are made in military and political hierarchies as well as distinct professions and classes of people within each culture. The differentiation of gender, obviously, plays an equally profound role in determining the ultimate shape of all things worn.

Sketch during construction of costumes for the film, "To Dream of Roses" (left), by Susan Nininger. Photo: Ann Marsden.

Etching of French nobleman c. 1630 (below), by Abraham Bosse.

Victoria Ridenour at her dressing table (opposite). Photo: Stephen Jacobson.

Costuming has always been a crucial element in the effective practice of religion and ceremony. From the Hopi kachina to the gods of Tibet, spiritual archetypes are made manifest with "masks and feathers." To this day, the magic of ritual is potent in any form because it is an expression of instinct. Simply by changing costumes, we can transform ourselves, explore new dimensions, gain new powers, discover new insights, and expand our awareness. This is ancient magic, part of our earthly inheritance, and a bridge to spirit worlds.

The elaborate traditions and repertoire of the theatre have their roots in the church, and rely heavily upon costuming for presentational effect. Most any actor will tell you that they do not fully *become* their character until they put on their costume and makeup. Costuming is such an important element that some directors dispense with sets entirely, allowing the costumes to establish the time and place of the drama. Other contemporary forms of entertainment continue to utilize the art of costuming—from the gut-level images in rock music videos to the high-tech robotic aliens of cinema.

Each of us, consciously or not, practices this art. Halloween, Mardi Gras, and formal rites of passage are obvious examples. Yet every day we exercise our choice of garb and fashion, thereby expressing something of our personality, mood, heritage, culture, and innermost being.

This book begins to document and celebrate a re-emergence of this rich art form. Being somewhat of an underground movement, and only vaguely recognized in the "fine arts," it is rapidly evolving and therefore difficult to present in a comprehensive manner. Yet it is hoped that this first book of its kind will add significantly to the growing practice of costumemaking, and its appreciation.

—Thom Boswell

The New Art of Costume—Art to Watch and Wear

by Janet Wilson Anderson

The stage is dark; the master of ceremonies announces, "The Spirit of the Greenwood," and the music surges. A spotlight hits the back of a tall woman, with foliage-entwined hair and cascades of intricate fabrics in leaf and bark patterns cloaking her body. She turns, then teases the audience, hiding the front of her costume while peering, owl-like, from behind her twiggy fingers. Finally, she spreads her arms wide and displays an elaborate trapunto and appliqué fabric sculpture of a full-sized tree. It is meticulously detailed, and its leaves sparkle vibrantly in the bright light. The audience audibly catches its breath at the sight. Jacqui Ward, costume artist, is on her way to winning Best in Show in the science fiction and fantasy masquerade competition at Costume Con, the annual costuming convention.

The past decade has seen the emergence of a new art form, one which confounds traditional categories, just as its practitioners and venues confound traditional artist, museum and gallery definitions. Its

practitioners call it "costuming" and themselves "costumers," but it is not what is commonly thought of by that term. It is not the costuming of stage or cinema, nor the special event costuming of Halloween, nor the scholarly research into historical costume, although the costume artist may do all of these as well. It is not necessarily the wearable art of the galleries, although much of the work is so well crafted that it is sometimes considered such. It is not the static costuming of the museum, shown on mannequins or frozen in cases. This new art of costuming is dynamic. It is not only displayed; it moves.

This type of costuming encompasses elements of theater, fashion, technology, and performance art, as well as traditional fiber arts, crafts, design and sewing skills. It is the imaginative development of visual characters, with the human body as the exhibiting vehicle. Even when worn off stage, these costumes are characterizations, demanding changes of posture, mannerisms, even style of speech in their wearers. It is a four-dimensional art: the 3-D of clothing sculpture plus the added dimension of movement through time and space. It is art to be watched as well as seen.

While costumers will "dress" for almost anything—historical ball, future fashion show, or just parading around the convention halls—this art form reaches its highest peak in competition. In competition, the costumer combines the display of the costume with a mini-theatrical presentation to create an interesting character for the audience and judges. The costume design must convey the key traits of the character portrayed, and, with music and/or narration to accompany movement, the costumer becomes a complete new entity, quite real and different from the normal self. For 30 seconds or perhaps a minute, the costumer evokes a universe, a situation, and a personality, and attempts to communicate this to the audience and judges. It is the gestalt composed of

body covering, movement and presentation that creates this new art in its fullest form.

In these pages you will find examples of this new art form. While that fourth dimension of presentation cannot be shown, you will be able to see the diversity of visual creativity these artists have brought forth. You will see works of outrageous imagination and painstakingly-researched reproduction. You will see solos, couples and groups, large stage-filling costumes and intimate examples of fastidious workmanship. You might see kings and queens, crustaceous aliens, movie stars and wild west heroes, among many others. There are assorted pantheons and mythological figures, robots and demons. There are works using lavish fabrics and those made of cardboard and duct tape. In the historical realm, there are exact replicas of period garments as well as historical interpretations and "retro fashion." Overall, there is unparalleled richness of imagination, craftsmanship, and originality of vision.

And who are these costume artists? A few, as one might expect, are costume or clothing professionals. They make their living designing and making costumes for theater, movies, schools, or community groups. There is a significant segment that designs and makes custom clothing, especially wedding and special occasion clothes. There are many more who earn at least a portion of their income in these pursuits.

But the vast majority of those who answer to the "costumer" description do it as a serious avocation. They are employed as teachers, small business owners, travel managers, writers, corporate executives, librarians, construction workers, tax accountants, and secretaries, to mention just a few. There is a large, technologically sophisticated contingent, with computer programmers, software designers, electronic engineers, and all kinds of scientists, who are often drawn to the "tech" end of costuming. With their

Sketch of "Zero-G Baby Ball," a design for futuristic infant wear, by Susan Lynn Toker.

input, some costumes now include elaborate LED patterns, fiber optics, voice-activated circuits and micro-chip controllers. Recent competition costumes have featured startling special effects such as glowing swords, sequenced lights in headdresses, even Tesla-generated lightning bolts.

Demographically, costumers range from young children to adults in their seventies, and some plan on staying active into their eighties and nineties! The newborn babies of costuming couples may be presented in appropriate costume on stage by proud parents just a few months after they are born. Few competitions are without a baby dressed as "Baby Dragon," "Minglet of Mongo" or "The Young Prince Henry." Child costumers may begin making their own costumes as young as two or three years old, and compete in their own division as Junior Costumers until age 13.

The majority of active costumers are, however, in the 18 to 49 year old age group, and most have been costuming for three to eight years. As a group, these people are considerably better educated and more literate than the general populace. College educations, even advanced degrees are common, as are substantial libraries. They tend to have lively, expansive minds and, when in company with those who share their love of the art form, enjoy detailed discussions on new techniques, new sources for materials, or even the best use of a particular plastic. It's not surprising that, with an avocation that places a premium on creativity, their interests outside costuming should be as wide-ranging as those within it. At a recent Costume Con, the conversation in the hospitality suite one evening covered favorite Wagnerian operas, desktop publishing, the asteroid theory of dinosaur extinction, and a lively debate on animal rights, as well as the more predictable discussion of boneless corset construction and flat-lining methods.

These costume artists do not compete in the customary juried shows of the "art" world. They compete on stage. These staged "masquerade"

competitions are surprisingly widespread, and cover many different types of costuming. The competitions, both independently sponsored and in conjunction with other types of conventions, are held on local, regional and international levels. They can be found in Britain, Australia, Canada and Japan as well as the USA. Across the United States and Canada, nearly every weekend there will be one or more masquerades taking place.

A local masquerade may draw 20 competitors; a big international competition several hundred. The audiences may range from a few hundred attendees to many thousands. Over the last ten years, literally thousands of people have built costumes, climbed up on stage and presented their work to admiring audiences around the world.

The genesis of this costuming movement had an unusual source—the world of science fiction and fantasy "fandom." For over fifty years, the fans of this literary genre have gathered at conventions. From the beginning, some fans paid honor to their favorite books or characters by attending conventions in costume. Dejah Thoris, Flash Gordon, even Frankenstein's Monster could be seen in the halls. Often there would be a special party with a costume parade so those who had gone to the effort of donning these could show them off. From there, it was a short step to awarding prizes for Most Beautiful, Most Creative, Most Humorous, etc. And in the fifties, a few folks began to add a bit of presentation. Still, it was all fairly low-key.

Then the TV show "Star Trek" took off in the late sixties. From a few hundred SF fans at a "world" science fiction convention, SF conventions swelled with costumed fans paying tribute to Star Trek, Star Wars, and other media phenomenon. The masquerade competition began to grow as well. By 1979 the Worldcon masquerade had over 130 entries, and nearly 200 participants.

But the level of costuming sophistication, with very few exceptions, was pretty low. Three developments of the

"Empress of Xandra," a 1953 sci-fi costume. Design, Construction & Model: Marjii Ellers. Photo: Al Elliott.

1980s changed this: the development of the skill division system, the start of Costume Con, and the establishment of the International Costumer's Guild.

Prior to 1981, competitions were classless. The first-time costumer had to compete head-to-head with those who had won many times. There was no separation by skill level: there was no competition "ladder" to climb. Then a skill division system—Novice, Journeyman, Master—based on the number of wins was proposed and first used at the 1981 Worldcon masquerade. Now, there was a clear upwards path of recognition based on accomplishment. Suddenly, beginning costumers felt protected and encour-

"Dread Warrior," a wrath-of-god futuristic warrior. Design, Construction & Model: Deborah Jones; Photo: John Upton—I.N.S.

aged to compete. Advanced costumers gained recognition as "Masters," but realized they would now have to stretch, since they were competing against others of similar advanced skills. As the use of the skill division system filtered down to regional and local SF conventions, overall costume quality soared.

In 1982 a seminal event happened. A group of costumers in San Diego decided to hold an independent convention, one devoted solely to the emerging costuming art. The first Costume Con had a heavy SF & Fantasy element, with an SF masquerade, future fashion design competition and future fashion show. But the committee chose to go beyond that base.

"Streamline Robot" (left), a sculpture by Toby Buonagurio, and further inspiration for "Dread Warrior." From a photo by Courtney Frisse.

The convention reached out to the historical costumers as well, with the first historical masquerade. It offered lots of general costuming programming on techniques and materials, plus exhibits, a dealers' room and social events. Even more importantly, it was the first time that people from all over the country identified themselves as "costumers," with a unique special interest. They began to learn and share with one another. A community was born.

In its infancy, this community was still rooted primarily in the world of science fiction fandom, only vaguely recognizing that there existed substantial interest in a wide variety of types of costuming. In 1985, the idea of an organized structure encompassing many types of costuming and costumers from many geographical areas coalesced into the International Costumer's Guild. A chapter-based organization, the ICG offered a framework for costumers to organize themselves, a way to get together, ex-

"Imperial Army Officer," Germany c. 1480 (right). Design & Construction: Elizabeth Pidgeon & Carl Ontis; Model: Carl Ontis; Photo: Stephen Jacobson.

"Court of the Peacock King." Design, Construction & Models: Kathy & Drew Sanders, Barb & Reg Schofield, Martin Miller, Caroline Julian, David Graham & Neola Caveny; Photo: John Upton— I.N.S.

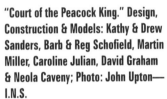

change ideas, work on projects and learn from each other. As Guild chapters formed, they tapped the unexpected wellspring of costuming fascination.

By Costume Con 8 in 1990, its sponsor, the West Coast chapter of the ICG, could draw on not only SF and fantasy costumers, but medievalists from the Society for Creative Anachronism, Renaissance Faire participants, ethnic and folk costumers, soldiers and their ladies from the Civil War reenactors, Victorian and Regency dancers, costume professors and their students from high schools and colleges, members of local theater groups, costume designers for the big amusement parks, television shows and film, not to mention a large number of folks who just liked to make and wear costumes. The synergy was terrific. The art form was expanding its boundaries and developing an astonishing range of amazing work.

So why do people do this? Costuming is not cheap in either time or money. Costumes competing in the international Master's class, the highest level of competition, may take three years in the planning, months in the construction and hundreds, if not thousands, of dollars to complete. Since the only reward of most competitions is peer acclaim and a certificate, it may be difficult to understand why so many people invest their time, money and talents in an activity that offers so little material reward.

Perhaps part of the explanation lies in the chance to externalize a rich fantasy life, to become for a short time the hero or villain of a long-ago age or far distant future. Or in part, it may be the chance to leave a mundane, somewhat drab existence behind and explore the sensuous pleasures of rich fabrics, jewels and trims. It may be the heady excitement of the audience's applause, the thrill of pure creativity or pleasure of peer recognition. Or it may be simpler still: the fun of "dressing up"; the joy of making others go "Oooooooo, look at that!"

Now, with a skill system to encourage participation, a Guild support network to foster community and informa-

tion exchange, and conventions devoted solely to the art, the costume artist works in a supportive, idea-rich environment. A costumer may specialize in one costume form or extend into many. But today no costumer need work completely alone; no one need pin up her own hem nor fit his own coat. The costuming community has become self-aware. And it has spawned a vibrant visual art form—one which continues to evolve and expand its practitioners, as well as delight a growing audience.

Gladiator from "Cabaret of the 21st Century." Design & Construction: Estelle Akamine; Photo: Sandy Clifford.

The Essence of Costumemaking

by Sha Sha Higby

Ah, the "greater costume" of the body...art that starts from the body, is suggested by the body, and inspired by the body.

Perhaps the artist doesn't like the reign of fashion, and has a more time-less vision. They love to make things, play with the sensation of materials, and see their costumes in the context of a fantastic effect or dramatic event.

They may be torn between sculpture and fashion: the body is the closest and most convenient inspiration to us, and is a natural base from which to work. It can animate itself through movement, forming new planes in the costume as it changes. Maybe it isn't wearable, but becomes a vessel for the body. Add the dimension of props and an environment, and this "greater costume of the body" becomes an even richer medium.

"The Tin Twin," a sculptural performance work. Design, Construction & Model: Sha Sha Higby; Photo: Albert Hollander.

If we would see ourselves as a melange of floating shapes and colors, intertwining and becoming more intricate, wrapping and knotting into tighter, brighter fists of color and texture that burst and release into other planes…Our bodies are composed of many tiny painter's canvases. As smoke curls and wafts through the air, all our thoughts flow and interconnect, floating and penetrating each other. If you were to draw these thoughts with pencils, illustrating their emotional meanings with abstract pictures and colors, blowing out and around an environment, how would you draw them? If they were sad thoughts, or excited thoughts…how would you draw them then?

Theatrical costume (opposite). Photo: Paul Jeremias.

"Paper Costume" (right). Design & Construction: Bae Jung Soon.

"The Night Porter" (below), by Victoria Ridenour. Photo: Stephen Jacobson.

As our bodies are moving paintings, every moment changing form and color, consider our limbs and fingers, too. You can affix extensions to the body. You can attach shapes, and experiment with how they move about in space. The costume artist faces the dilemma of making intriguing, yet sturdy and comfortable methods of attaching these costume components to the body. They have to hold up to the thrashings of movement—even rain! (How washable and reusable are these costumes, and what nightmares must dry-cleaners face?)

Some of these sculptural costumes are sacred to the artist, and incur more spirit each time they are worn. Each of the artists in the following pages cut, sewed, glued, painted, and sculpted fragments of interpretations of their lives that could not otherwise be seen—like an aura. Or perhaps they are costumes that resulted from the surprises of working with certain materials, and a longing for something else.

Drawing of "Mermaid Ambassador," by Animal X.

Now you make a costume: Feel the blood spinning through your body, and imagine that you become an immense landscape. The tip of your chin is a steep and dangerous cliff, your eyelashes are tall feathery trees, there are gentle valleys in the lavender recesses of your eyes, and your ears are darkened, mossy caves. Silver crystals fill your spinning pulse, and twinkle. How does your head hinge into the sky? The ends of your fingers grow finely spun silk threads. Your body is hollow, except for something strangely new inside. Your whole body is splitting softly and peeling apart into the grasses, and you can't help it. You are surrounded by thousands of colorful molecules that push against you and hold you up. They are happy little molecules that laugh as they push themselves against you. Perhaps some part of you feels discomfort. Search for the edges of that discomfort. Make a drawing of it, and give it color and shape. How far does it go into your body? What are the different temperatures of your body, and does the heat radiate out further in some parts than others? What is the design and shape of each ray? With your fingers, touch the edges of how far the heat reaches all around your neck, head, and out of your ears. What is the design of that heat? Does it have a certain color? Do the colors blend gradually from one shade to the next? Are there an assortment of shapes that bubble out, long and thin? Or do their roots reach inside of you, like oceans of tiny colorful fish that reflect new temperatures and colors as they flow between the island recesses of your body? You can mold and shape these forms that float in and out as you move about in space. Are they simple shapes or complex, vast or intricate, opaque or transparent, weighted or light, rough or smooth? You might try imagining these qualities as you first lift out of bed in the morning.

See how primal, natural, and easy it is to make a costume! Move along with it, and imagine the environment that it might live in. Even if you have made a costume for your little finger, you'll be surprised how easily it can grow to encompass your entire body—even adding on parts to enhance its form and movement. Explore it; bring it to life.

Now, add the dimension of performance. Imagine your body extended to the outermost edges of the costume you have made. Feel the sensations of becoming a new being. In Japanese Noh theatre, there is a ritual for donning the mask which triggers the moment of transformation.

Some costumers present their work without performance. Yet even as a fine art "installation" in a gallery or museum, a costume can project its own character, intension and environment. Here, effective placement and lighting become especially important.

Each artist's approach is a little different, because they are all different beings who love to experiment with the behaviors and effects of different materials and movements. And yet a finished costume will also take on a life of its own, and determine how you might act and move. It could be considered a mask, but it often has more to do with the fantasy and fun that startlingly evokes deeper meaning, simply because we are completely involved and enjoying ourselves beautifully.

Detail of "Music Box Dancer." Design, Construction & Model: Wendy Ross; Photo: Linda Sweeting.

HISTORIC

VICTORIA RIDENOUR &
ADRIAN BUTTERFIELD

I think all successful costumers have to have a strong streak of the romantic in them. Being a professional and sewing for a living, I'm sometimes overwhelmed by the more mundane aspects of costuming: running a business, paying the bills…The opportunity to put on a costume and become somebody else is irresistible. It keeps costuming fun.

Each costume we design and make has a person behind it. That's why detail is so important to us. Clothes need to be real from the skin out so you can live the character you portray. As soon as you cross the boundary from "dress-up" to putting on the person as well as the clothes, it's easy. Going on stage as Titania, Elric, or whomever, is completely believable when you have a foundation to base your actions upon. The costume is part of you.

"Sir Colin" (right), cavalier court suit. Design & Construction: Adrian Butterfield; Model: Tim Bray; Photo: Stephen Jacobson.

"Georgian Robe Francaise" (opposite left). Design, Construction & Model: Victoria Ridenour; Photo: Stephen Jacobson.

"Elizabethan Court Gown" (right). Design, Construction & Model: Victoria Ridenour; Photo: Stephen Jacobson.

Victoria at her dressing table (bottom right). Photo: Stephen Jacobson.

"Gentleman's Suit,"
c. 1820 (right). Design,
Construction & Model:
Adrian Butterfield;
Photo: Stephen
Jacobson.

"Early Victorian Day Dress" (above). Design,
Construction & Model: Victoria Ridenour;
Photo: Stephen Jacobson.

"Postillion," c. 1855 (right). Design,
Construction & Model: Victoria Ridenour;
Photo: Stephen Jacobson.

See page 62 for artist's statement.

"Napoleonic Court Dress," c. 1806 (above). Design, Construction & Model: Janet Wilson Anderson; Photo: John Youden.

"Ascot Dress" from the movie "My Fair Lady" (left). Design: Cecil Beaton; Construction & Model: Janet Wilson Anderson; Photo: David Bickford.

21

LITA SMITH-GHARET

I don't think I had much of a choice but to be influenced by animal hide and natural materials. I spent most of my childhood living on the Yakima Indian Reservation and was surrounded by incredible works of beading on leather. When I was a little older I married a leather-wearin' Harley rider. I always knew just what to make him.

For years I've been carving fossilized Woolly Mammoth Ivory, bones and antlers. This assortment sure comes in handy when I'm making buttons and jewelry to accent the furs and leather in my costumes.

I've designed and constructed costumes for all sorts of entertainers: muzzel-loaders, Indian dancers, the Society of Creative Anachronism, belly dancers, showgirls, actors, the costuming community, and just for fun.

I also enjoy beading and wearing evening gowns, but it just can't top the smell and feel of real leather.

Primitive clothing fashioned from animal skins, ivory and lapidary. Design, Construction & Model: Lita Smith-Gharet.

KENNETH ALLEN

My costumes have been made primarily for wearing in New York City's Village Halloween Parade. Walking costumed at night on the streets of the Big Apple is a wonderful experience. I am continually amazed at the number of Manhattanites who, no matter how outrageously I am dressed, can walk by without any apparent reaction! At the other end of the spectrum, no matter how esoteric my costume, I've overheard people in the crowd recognize it. ("There goes Quetzalcoatl!") The first time I wore Tezcatlipoca (the jaguar) Kurt Vonnegut, the author, rushed up to me and said, "You're a Meso-American god of war, right?" Then again, when I wore Zochipilli (the eagle) someone asked, "What are you, a turkey?" So it goes. My costumes are actually offerings of appreciation for the privilege of being able to live in this extraordinary city.

"Tzcoatlipoca (jaguar)," Aztec god of young warriors (above). Design, Construction & Model: Kenneth Allen; Photo: Mariette Pathy Allen.

"Quetzalcoatl (plumed serpent)," Aztec god of learning (left). Credits, same as left.

"Xochipilli (eagle)," Aztec god of flowers and dance (right). Credits: same as above.

BARB SCHOFIELD

Costuming is a creative outlet that can be as simple or complex, and as expensive or inexpensive, as the costumer wishes. Costuming's many forms provide an alternative experience to life's daily routine, and offer something for every taste and experience level. The primary rewards of costuming are to be found in the joy of creation—not in awards won.

"Shadows of the Terror: Friday the 13th, 1789" (above). Design & Construction: Barb Schofield; Models: Barb Schofield & Martin Miller; Photo: John Upton—I.N.S.

"Lady Calitha" (left). Design, Construction & Model: Barb Schofield; Photo: Linda Sweeting.

"The Legacy of Power" (opposite). Design & Construction: Barb Schofield & Mary Hudson; Models: Jan Finder, Laurel Cunningham-Hill, Mary Hudson, Barb Schofield & Richard Hill; Photo: Linda Sweeting.

THE SOFT TOUCH

We are a fifteen-year-old collective of artists who make wearable art and operate our own store in San Francisco. We inspire and amuse ourselves by creating costumes, many of which we incorporate into our daily dress. "This is not a costume—this is my clothing."

We designed and created these costumes as a group process. Starting with the concept of coronation robes for Macbeth and Lady Macbeth, we made them in sections— each choosing the parts that most inspired us. We gave Macbeth a capelet in the shape of a wolf skin and put the forest (Birnam Wood) on his crown. Lady Macbeth has those elusive babies on her sleeve, and drops of blood (red crystal beads) dangling from the fabric claws that adorn her collar. To preserve the sensitive lamés, we covered them with sheer fabrics and created a whole new world of metallic effects, which we've used many times since.

For us, costuming is a living art. It feeds our obsession to decorate. Our motto is: "No such thing as too much."

"The King and Queen of Swords." Design & Construction: Gail Alien, Robin Lewis, João Soares, Stan Hite, Charlotte Davis, Jackie Cabasso & Rosemarie Bolte; Photos: Peter Villums.

JWLHYFER DE WINTER

I seek, by wearing costumes, to invoke the magical, fairy-tale part of myself. I believe that other realms do exist and that creating and wearing costumes is one way to evoke these realms.

Wearing costumes as part of my everyday dress, I become a walking piece of art. Every person who sees the character I have created is touched in some way. It is lovely to help people remember the magical, innocent, child-like part of themselves. It inspires them to be more adventurous in their own dress.

This is the most incredible time in the history of dress, in a way, because we have access to so much information and are not limited in what we can wear by class consciousness. Even artists of limited means can express themselves through "fancy dress," and rise above circumstance. Most of my costumes are put together out of thrift-store finds and other remnants. I don't think I could have done that a hundred years ago.

"Elizabethan Gown from the wardrobe of Lady Sibyl Whitaker" (right). Design, Construction & Model: Jwlhyfer de Winter; Photo: Stephen Jacobson.

"Mary Shelley's Day Dress, and Mary's Pelise-robe & Bonnet" (right). Design & Construction: Jwlhyfer de Winter; Models: Jwlhyfer & Kira Lentaigne; Photo: John Williams, at Mary Shelley's mother's grave in Camden Town.

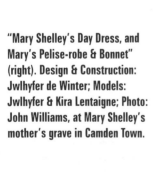

"Renaissance Wedding Regency Costume" (far right). Design, Construction & Model: Jwlhyfer de Winter; Photo: John Williams, at Audley End House, Essex.

"Thrift store fantasy Rococo Masquerade" (below). Design, Construction & Model: Jwlhyfer de Winter; Photo: Barron Scott Levkoff.

"Ophelia's Dress" (above), a pre-Raphaelite gown. Design, Construction & Model: Jwlhyfer de Winter; Photo: John Williams, at Kelmscott Manor, Oxfordshire, former home of William Morris and Dante Gabriel Rossetti.

LANI TUCKER

I dance with the OTE'A Polynesian Folk Ensemble. Our "Old Style" costumes are well-researched recreations which we make as authentically as possible. "No matter how pretty it is, if it didn't come from that island, you can't use it on that costume."

Most Polynesian royalty were large people. The bigger you were, the more "mana" (spirit power) you had, plus, the commoners could see you coming. Also, fair skin was a status symbol—tattoos showed up well on it.

They liked to decorate their bodies with almost anything within reach: flowers, greenery, seeds, fruit, shells, teeth, feathers…They made cloth (tapa) from beaten bark, which could be plain, dyed, painted or stamped with designs, even scented with plumeria blossoms and the like. The standard garment for both genders was the "pareo," which could be worn as a dress, skirt, pants, poncho, shawl, or whatever.

"Samoan Princess," pre-World War II (above). Design, Construction & Model: Lani Tucker, headdress by Kaycee Dewar; Photo: Stephen Jacobson.

"Tahitian Woman of High Rank," c. 1800 and the voyages of Captain Cook (left). Credits: same as above.

30

PATRICIA RICKARD

I specialize in period costumes. Whether it's the challenge of recreating a piece from a portrait, or executing my own design, I am known for my ability: "If I can draw it, I can make it."

As always, my best work is still on the sewing machine. Currently, I'm working on the entire Royal Swedish Court, which will be presented at a local Renaissance Faire.

Period Gown (left), designed, made and modelled by Patricia Rickard.

Period characters aboard ship (below), designed, made and modelled by the ensemble, and Sean Willee.

JANA KEELER

I believe in costuming from the skin out: correct underpinnings, hairstyles and makeup. Each period I do elicits different feelings about the woman I have created, and wearing this "clothing" gives me a deep respect for how our foremothers lived. I realize how much luckier I am when, at the end of a long day, I can take off my corset and fall into a nice pair of sweats.

Although I have designed and executed many costumes from scratch, it can be very expedient and cost-effective to rework existing costume pieces, as illustrated by the costumes shown here.

"English Renaissance," c. 1560 (left). Design, Construction & Model: Jana Keeler; Photo: Stephen Jacobson.

"The Blue Ballgown," c. 1850 (above). Design: Stephanie Galicia; Construction & Model: Jana Keeler. "Red Suit," 16th C. Design & Model: Neil Hudner; Construction: Sandy Tremblay. "Shakespeare." Design & Construction: Shaun Otey; Model: Gregory Bell. Photo: Stephen Jacobson.

CHERIE MOORE

I have been sewing ever since I was about five years old. I made clothing for my dolls by copying the 17th century clothing in my Mother Goose book. I started using period patterns, and gradually became more meticulous about historical accuracy.

Into my teens, I had plans of becoming a veterinarian. But as I was sitting at my sewing machine one day, wondering what direction my life should take, it dawned on me: making costumes is what I am really good at. Now I participate in the Renaissance Faire, the Dickens Christmas Faire, Period Costumed Balls, and various Costume Conventions.

If I had my way, I would wear my costumes every day. I have always felt that I was born in the wrong century.

"Evening Gown," c. 1896 (above). Design, Construction & Model: Cherie Moore; Photo: Wendy Dean.

"Ball Gown," c. 1904 (right). Credits: same as above.

ANIMAL X

See page 42 for artist's statement.

"Lord and Lady Lovecraft" (right). Design &
Construction: Animal X; Models: Eric Blackburn
& Animal X; Photos: Stephen Jacobson.

"Lady Hawke." Design & Construction: Animal X;
Model: Lorraine Sturges; Photo: Stephen Jacobson.

"Vanity (from the Seven Deadly Sins)" emerges from her
grandiose bustle that is actually a (vanity) dressing table,
singing "I feel pretty…" Design, Construction & Model:
Animal X; Photos: John Upton—I.N.S.

"The Black Adder & Queen Elizabeth" (below), from the popular BBC television series that infused the "sword and sorcery" genre with comic overtones. Design & Construction: Angelique Trouvere; Models: Angelique Trouvere & Kristopher Curling (courtesy of Doctors in the House); Photo: Mark Harju.

JENNIFER TIFFT

See page 106 for artist's statement.

"Mary Elizabeth Bainbridge."
Design, Construction & Model: Jennifer Tifft;
Photo: Michelyn Monson.

JEANNETTE HOLLOMAN

The "African Tudor" is a historical recreation combining two distinctive design elements: English Tudor silhouette, fabric and color, with African craftsmanship and decoration. The underskirt is smocked velvet and is studded with Egyptian style scarabs. The bodice piece has a style of embroidery from the central Niger region of Wodaabe, shisha mirrors, stained glass drops representing amber from the Mali region and fresh water pearls. Jewelry includes a Cowrie shell anklet, a Mud fish necklace of Asante design (a symbol of help, nourishment and protection), beads, and an amber ring. The headdress is of Zaire origin and is made of wire wrapped with lace and painted gold, interspaced with earrings.

"African Tudor." Malawi, daughter of an Ivory Coast trader, sails to England and will be presented at court in this gown. Design: Jennifer Ketcham & Jeannette Holloman; Construction & Photo: Jennifer Ketcham; Model: Jeannette Holloman.

Members of the Civil War Association at Fort Tejon, California. Photos: Stephen Jacobson.

At its simplest, it's a guy in jeans and a cowboy hat "plinking" with a kit-built muzzle-loaded derringer. At its most obsessive, it's knowing that every stitch in your holsters is done in flax—not cotton thread. At its worst, it's duct tape swords and armor with the attitude of "If they'd had it then, they would've used it." And at its best, it's being the gun-captain of a Confederate six-pound Napoleon canon, facing down 3,000 massed Union troops on the original battlefield. That is reenacting.

14th U.S. Infantry, Company A

Ladies' Auxilliary

ELIZABETH PIDGEON & CARL ONTIS

When I first met Carl he was wearing nothing but long-johns and holding a coffee cup, standing by a campfire at a "Rendezvous." I wasn't impressed. But when he transformed himself into a Crow warrior c. 1840's, I changed my mind.

We do costuming for a variety of reasons. We participate in a variety of living history reenactments at historic sites, a 19th-century wild west show, and historical film work. There are also costume conventions, history symposiums, black powder rendezvous, single-action shooting events, ethnic and early dance groups, and themed weekends hosted by various groups.

If we do costuming for a variety of reasons, we do research for one reason: we enjoy it. Learning how someone would have dressed is integral to "walking a mile in their shoes."

"True Girls of the West" (below). Redesigned, Reconstructed & Worn by Elizabeth Pidgeon-Ontis & Aurie Bradley.

"Pawnee Bill & his Beautiful Bevy of Buckaroo Bimbos" (right). Design, Construction & Models: Carl Ontis, Cathie Berté & Elizabeth Pidgeon-Ontis; Photo: Stephen Jacobson.

"Comanche Dress," c. 1833. Reproduction & Model: Elizabeth Pidgeon-Ontis.

Carl's been involved in researching, collecting and making Western & Indian costumes for over 20 years. He's encouraged me to research and learn obscure techniques like porcupine quillwork. We believe that good work deserves good materials. One's time being the greater investment in any project, only the most appropriate materials should ever be used. This is where stage costume and historical clothing depart from each other, "appropriate" being relative to the purpose of the costume.

In historical costuming, people talk about reproduction versus interpretation with great fervor. The level of research required for interpretation is general, while reproduction requires intense levels of research into precise construction techniques. Both are valid approaches, and both are costume.

"Crow Indian," c. 1850 (below).
Reproduction & Model: Carl Ontis.

"Piegan Dress," c. 1840 (right).
Reproduction & Model: Elizabeth Pidgeon-Ontis.

CAROLYN SALEMI

The first costumes I made as a child were American Indian, based on the Ben Hunt Boy Scout books. I was so intense, my parents kept telling me I must be a reincarnated Indian. My later costumes were theatre related.

During college, I dated several Native Americans. I made some really nice "regalia" and started going to a lot of Pow Wows to learn more, dance competitively, and socialize.

"Arapaho Dress," c. 1850. Reproduction & Model: Carolyn Salemi; Photo: John Upton—I.N.S.

After college I was an art teacher and a consultant on Native American cultures for the Mid Hudson Valley region. Costume Conventions finally gave me a format to use all my skills and interests in a short theatrical setting.

"Oklahoma Fancydancer." Design & Construction: Carolyn Salemi & Steve GreyMorning; Model: Steve GreyMorning; Photo: Cas. Salemi.

JEANNIE TRIMMER

Most of my costumes are based on actual historic designs. But after looking at a number of paintings from an era, I combine the aspects I like the best.

This costume started as a simple Middle-Eastern dance costume. It was inspired by all of the wonderful/awful *Sinbad* movies ever made, as well as the 1940's version of *Kismet*, and is based very loosely on actual historical designs from medieval Persia, mixed heavily with Hollywood styling.

While this is still a work in progress, I love wearing it to dance in—especially since so many people think of all Middle-Eastern dancers as belly dancers in beaded bras and gauze skirts.

"Scheherezade—the early days." Design, Construction & Model: Jeannie Trimmer; Photo: Bill Trimmer.

MELA HOYT-HEYDON & FRIENDS

In this day and age of instant gratification, disposable goods, and trendy conformity, historical costuming challenges me to create clothing with skill and pride. As a professional costume designer, most of my friends enjoy making creative clothing, too. When we design and make costumes for ourselves, there are no restrictions. By wearing our creations, we can escape the stresses of the present and enjoy the pleasant pastimes of bygone eras. We get together at historical picnics, teas, balls, and weekend-long events to show off our craft, share our skills, and simply have a good time. Our period functions have spanned from the Middle Ages to the Roaring Twenties, but currently the Victorian Era is our favorite venue.

"Victorian Tea Party." Design, Construction & Models (l–r): Joyce Morris, Cynthia Harris, Mela Hoyt-Heydon & Celeste Moring; Photo: Stephen Jacobson.

FANTASTIC

When people ask me why that's my name, I tell them, "You'd have to watch me eat." And, yes, I'm very proud of my pink hair, which I've had since 1976. I like to think that if some hair really was pink, that would be my color.

I grew up in California, trained as an illustrator, and work as a costumer. I've made outfits for people like Madonna, David Bowie, Diana Ross, and Kiss, and have done a few "weirdo" walk-on parts on movies. But for fun, I make my own costumes for costume conventions and historical reenactment groups. I also enjoy working with the younger school kids—they still *believe* in fantasy.

I've been billed as a "performance artist." I'm not too crazy about that term, but it *has* gotten me some grants. I like to utilize music—sometimes my own compositions—and even dance in my costume presentations. My performances are simple, direct, and full of strong emotion. I believe that ART is making people feel what you want them to feel.

"Rapture of the Deep" (left). Mother Ocean and her children, performing for Earth Day. Design, Construction & Model: Animal X; Photo: John Upton—I.N.S.

"To Believe in the Good in Man." Gaiea (shown above), in her organic earthly splendor, is confronted by Mankind (not shown), portrayed in harsh synthetic garb. Design, Construction & Model: Animal X; Photo: Linda Sweeting.

Back View

"The Color of White" (opposite left) is a ribbon wedding dress. Design, Construction & Model: Animal X; Photo: Stephen Jacobson.

"Holocaust—the Demon Within" (bottom). Design, Construction & Model: Animal X.

"Tribute" (left) to Robert Heinlein. Design, Construction & Model: Animal X.

"Aurora Borealis, Empress of the Northern Lights" (below) is self-illuminated with fiber optics and changes colors. Design, Construction & Model: Animal X; Photo: Stephen Jacobson.

I am a costumer because it's fun! Many of my embellishments and decoration are like doodling with a needle and thread.

Living in the Virgin Islands, I am out of the mainstream, so my costumes tend to be a little different. Most of my characters are inhabitants of the imaginary country of Drusba ("absurd" spelled backwards).

I wish I had more opportunities to wear my costumes. Finding the materials I need is a challenge here as well. I compete with the local "ladies of the night" for the most exotic finds at the only flea market on the island.

"Bride of the Ice Demon" (below). Design, Construction & Model: Julia Ann Hyll; Photo: David Cover.

"Fire God." Design, Construction & Model: Julia Ann Hyll; Photo: Linda Sweeting.

"A Wizard & his Apprentice Meet the Ambassador from Drusba" (above). Design & Construction: Julia Ann Hyll; Models: Julia Ann Hyll & husband; Photo: David Cover.

"Mistress of Ritual Magic" (opposite). Design, Construction & Model: Julia Ann Hyll; Photo: David Cover.

I've taught art in public schools since 1967. I started costuming with elaborate makeup and prosthetics but had to give that up due to sensitive skin. So I started making masks and costumes to go with them, first with papier-mâché. That was because it was cheap, easy to work with, and could be made strong but light. I have also worked extensively in latex slush and foam castings (very expensive). I have full hydrocal replicas of my head, hands and feet, so I can come up with a lot of great variations and make complete head-to-toe costumes.

I have always enjoyed creating weird aliens and creatures. I have also done recreations and am now venturing into historical costuming. I costume for teaching workshops, competitions, gaming societies, and occasionally openings and promotions for movies.

"Neek" (opposite left), from "The Explorers." Design, Construction & Model: Vandy Vandervort; Photo: Greg Bradt.

"Maiden from Mer" (opposite right), inspired by the surrealist Magritte. Credits: same as above.

"Augra" (right), from "The Dark Crystal." Credits: same as above.

ROBIN LEWIS

I think of myself as a sort of shy exhibitionist—not theatrical, but addicted to beautiful images. The image of wings especially appeals to me, and the articulation of scales is fascinating. I love the idea of expressing such natural forms with simple shapes that, when combined, convey them fully. I am intrigued with the image of armor. I call some of my pieces "soft armor." I like that they are comfortable and sensual to touch, but also protective and evocative of strength and power.

"Lizard Armor" (opposite bottom). Design & Construction: Robin Lewis; Model: Ellen Jo Kash; Photo: Paul Reeberg.

"Rainbow Bird" (opposite top). Design, Construction & Model: Robin Lewis; Photo: Robert Pruzan.

"Silver Warrior, Lizard Armor & Space Traveller" (left). Design & Construction: Robin Lewis & Gail Alien; Models: Sarah Shriver, Ellen Jo Kash & Inga Williams; Photo: Paul Reeberg.

"Shadow Puppet" (below). Design, Construction & Model: Robin Lewis; Photo: Paul Reeberg.

DENICE GIRARDEAU

One of my earliest memories is the intense envy I felt for some neighbors' Halloween costumes made by their mother, when my three sisters and I had to make do with chintzy storebought outfits.

More than any other hobby I've had (and there've been plenty), costuming allows such freedom for experimentation that it encompasses everything I've ever learned as far as arts and crafts.

My costumes start from many different places—a color combination, the imaginary feel of a skirt sweeping out behind me, a half-remembered dream, a dance. Quite often my inspiration comes from a desire to make people screw up their faces and wonder "What the hell…?!"

"Magma Pele Volcana" (above). Design, Construction & Model: Denice Girardeau; Photo: Chip Clark.

"Carmoon Mirandroid" (right). Design, Construction & Model: Denice Girardeau; Photo: Linda Sweeting.

52

I'm an actress who can't memorize lines. So parading around in a fancy costume that can speak for itself is the next best thing.

But perhaps even more, I love designing the line, the detailings, figuring out the construction, searching out and gathering the materials, drafting the pattern and then—heart-stopping moment!—cutting into the fabric itself (especially if it cost more than $20 a yard!).

"Empire Formal" (bottom left). Design, Construction & Model: Sally Fink; Photo: Chip Clark.

"Return of the Iron Orchid" (bottom right). Design, Construction & Model: Sally Fink; Photo: Linda Sweeting.

Drawings by Sally Fink.

For fifteen years I made costumes for competition at science fiction conventions and futuristic fashion shows. Strictly for stage wear, many of them were not comfortable. But I was always so excited the night of the competition, I didn't feel the weight of headpieces or the monofilament line cutting into my flesh.

Now I design costumes for characters in the novels I'm writing. Often the costume makes a story point, or even plays an integral part in the plot. The psychology of dress fascinates me and is reflected in my stories. I hope someday to see the costumes in my books translated into cloth by other costuming fans.

Costuming brings a little glamour into my life. The kinds of costumes I design would be for a person of power and influence, of which I have very little in real life.

Most of my costumes begin as full-length, T-shaped tunics, but when trims, jewelry, and various kinds of over-drapings are added, they look more complex than they are. My design inspiration is mostly Oriental and Central Asiatic, with a touch of Plains Indian. European styles are too fussy, frilly, and puffy for my taste.

My attitude toward jewelry is akin to the ancient Egyptians (clothes should be no more than a subtle background for gorgeous jewelry), and the Byzantines (if you've got it, flaunt it). Even my daily attire consists of Oriental-style tunics with slacks and conspicuous jewelry. It's very comfortable, and it makes me feel good.

"Imperial Cat-keeper of the Outer Regions" (opposite). Design, Construction & Model: Karen Kuykendall; Photo: John Aulick.

"Cat Warrior" (above). Credits: Same as above.

"The Firecat" (right). Credits: Same as above.

Until after my children were born, I never thought of myself as artistic. Somehow, however, I had always managed to produce costumes using existing clothes, glue, paint, and whatever strange objects seemed appropriate. I even occasionally did battle with my sewing machine to modify or create a necessary piece.

As my work gains in sophistication, I may be found bending pipe, doing fabric painting and dyeing, making foam prosthetics, playing with thermoplastics, working with papier-mâché, acrylics, caulking, wire, wield-

"The Three Furies" (above). Design: Dana MacDermott; Construction: Dana MacDermott, Lissa Daniels, Sidney Rice & Samantha Ash; Models: Stephanie Silverman, Sidney Rice & Maraba Hansill; Photo: Robert Graham.

"Athena" (right). Design: Dana MacDermott; Construction: Dana MacDermott, Dafni Kalogianni & Joan Cathcart; Model: Lisa Pearson; Photo: Robert Graham.

"Apollo" (opposite top). Design: Dana MacDermott; Construction: Dana MacDermott, Skipper Skeoch & Joan Cathcart; Model: Joshua Barnes; Photo: Robert Graham.

"Beneath Alien Waves" (opposite bottom). Design: Dana MacDermott; Construction: Dana & Bruce MacDermott & Friends; Models: Dana & Bruce MacDermott, Jaron Hollander; Photo: Michael Jhon.

ing a glue gun or a soldering iron, sitting at my drafting table or (God forbid) operating a sewing machine or serger. I generally work with a team (usually with my husband), both for the creative dynamics and so that the needed areas of expertise in construction are available.

I am enamored of texture, form and movement, and tend toward impressionism in my undertakings. I am happiest with the unexpected, with the non-human found in science fiction, and I often administer a dose of social commentary. Certainly there is a strong escapist element. Those of us who indulge in this art form postulate that there are alternative realities—even magic.

I tend to lose my objectivity about two-thirds of the way into a project.

Fortunately, the creative act has a way of manufacturing energy that fuels efforts long after the initial conviction has been consumed by the process. It is an infectious energy. My husband, Bruce, is the structural engineer for our projects. My son, Ari, has created sophisticated presentation sound tracks, and my younger son, Jaron, contracted the life-long disease of Theatre from his first exposure on the 1984 World Science Fiction Convention stage. Friends and acquaintances, and even casual visitors, have been drawn into our sewing and construction efforts.

My personal world has changed as a result of costuming. I am working toward an MFA in Costume and Set Design, and envision my future as a combination of teaching and design.

OFF THE WALL

"Off the Wall" was a truly collaborative undertaking, although each individual assumed primary responsibility for completing the egg they modeled. Once Humpty Dumpty was selected as our starting point, the serious nonsense began in earnest. All the costumed eggs have bow ties, something approximating suspenders, and shorts. Beyond that, we drew from the visual vocabulary of our chosen designers. We laughed at every stage.

"Bob Mackie" (left), by Alys Hay.

"Erté" (bottom left), by Dana MacDermott.

"Yves Saint Laurent" (below), by Bruce MacDermott.

58

"Claire Griffen—Mad Max" (top left),
by John Youden.

"Steve Silver—Beach Blanket Babylon"
(top right), by Julie Neff.

"Issey Miyake" (left), by Randy Neff.

All photos by Linda Sweeting.

TWEEDLE DEE

See page 40 for artist's statement.

"Medusa," before and after beheading. Design, Construction & Model: Carolyn Salemi; Photos: Linda Sweeting.

The Irish and Scottish legends of the Banshee (Bean Sidhe) have always fascinated me: the mournful woman, dead before her time, warning the living that their time has come. I wanted my Banshee to appear lovely and haunting, then change suddenly into a terrifying demon.

To achieve this effect, I used cool blues and greens which glowed enchantingly in regular light. But when the lighting shifts to ultra-violet, she shimmers, ghastly and surreal. When even the "black lights" are extinguished, all that is visible is a menacing specter, outlined with phosphorescent paint and batter-powered eye-bulbs, glowing red.

"Banshee," in two of her aspects.
Design, Construction & Model: Rae Bradbury;
Photo (above): Linda Sweeting;
Photo (left): Mark Leber.

I can't remember a time when I didn't wear costumes or have an interest in clothes, fashion, theatre, and pretty wearables. As a professional, I've spent the last fourteen years in the cosmetics end of the fashion game. And as a hobby, I've been involved with costuming and competitions.

In a costume, I can be different people, from different places and times. Part of it, too, is the joy of creating what I unabashedly call art. Costuming demands a creative inspiration, a technical expertise, a knowledge of design, line and form as much as any other art form. In its presentational form, it requires stage sense, evolution through time and space, and a mastery of body movement unlike any static form. It is a mix of sculpture and theater wrapped around a body.

There is a simple aesthetic side of it as well. In a world of power suits, T-shirts, and sweats, it is a pleasing diversion to run my hands over velvet, drip rhinestones through my fingers and let my eyes run riot in the brocades, lamés and sequins and to create from them something beautiful.

If there is a master theme in my costume design or construction, it is a love of the beautiful. I do all kinds of costumes—but I don't do ugly. I do pretty ladies, grand queens and kings, elegant dancers, fashionable business women, flirts and sexpots, glittery Vegas showgirls, handsome dandies, dashing officers, and ravishing courtesans. As a costumer, I'm an optimist; I like to make my world a lovelier place.

"Ritual Dancer, or The Wedding Cake Chandelier" (above). Design, Construction & Model: Janet Wilson Anderson; Photo: Linda Sweeting.

"King & Queen of the Spider Court" (left). Design & Construction: Janet Wilson Anderson; Models: Janet Wilson Anderson & Gary Anderson; Photo: Stephen Jacobson.

"Dalliance" (opposite), a venture into the Theatre of the Macabre. Design, Construction & Models: Janet Wilson Anderson, Robin Schindler & Joyce Best; Photo: Linda Sweeting.

WENDY ROSS

As a result of my earlier training as a fashion designer, I pursued my love for the interaction of fabric and the human body. The number of emotions that a garment can elicit is infinite. With costuming, there is a broader pallet

"Thetis, Goddess of the Waves" (left).
Design, Construction & Model: Wendy Ross;
Photo: Linda Sweeting.

"Selene, Goddess of the Night" (above).
Credits: same as above.

with which to work. In this unrestrained form of clothing, the imagination can call up virtually anything.

Most of my work is influenced by the fantasy worlds where faeries and elves abide. I combine hand-painted fabrics with hand beading and embroidery to create wearable art with a fanciful twist.

The art of costume should be a delight to the eye. Texture and color should combine to create interesting forms that draw one into the idea or character being represented. Both the wearer and observer should derive enjoyment from experiencing the costume. Some of the fun should be found in the exploration of a different idea or way of viewing the world. A costume can help transport the wearer into a world the artist seeks to create.

"Frost Faerie"
(right). Credits: same.

"Woodland Faerie"
(below). Credits: same.

"Music Box Dancer" (far left). Design, Construction & Model: Wendy Ross; Photo: Linda Sweeting.

"Wood Nymph" (left). Credits: same as above.

"Centaur" (below). Credits: same as above.

JENNIFER KETCHAM

The first time I remember noticing costumes as an expression of an artist's vision was when I saw Jean Cocteau's *Beauty and the Beast*. A fairy tale had literally come to life for me. Many things have influenced my costuming, but this film established a goal and a standard for me as to the level of artistry, detail, and narrative elements that costumes can contain, and the effect that they can have on the observer.

I approach all my costumes as individual art pieces that are going to be viewed from all angles. This influences every choice I make: the fabrics, the cut, the silhouette, and the trim added on to that. Light and shadow become important elements as well. I like costumes that have a lot of visual texture: over-layers of organza and chiffon, lace embroidered with pearls in the negative space, quilted and puckered velvet punctuated with stones. By layering and hanging things from the costumes, the fabric itself achieves a distinctive motion—even sound.

"Titania, Queen of the Fairies." Design & Drawing by Jennifer Ketcham.

"Summer Morning." Design, Construction & Model: Jennifer Ketcham; Makeup: Doug Clayton; Photo: Chip Clark.

"Italian Renaissance," c. 1480. Design, Construction & Model: Jennifer Ketcham; Photo: John Ketcham.

VICTORIA RIDENOUR & ADRIAN BUTTERFIELD

See page 18 for artist's statement.

A scene from "Midsummer Night's Dream" (opposite top). Design: Victoria Ridenour; Construction: Victoria Ridenour & Adrian Butterfield; Models: Greg Bevington & Gayle Hutchins; Photo: Stephen Jacobson.

"Titania & Oberon, from Midsummer Night's Dream" (below). Design, Construction & Models: Victoria Ridenour & Adrian Butterfield; Photo: Stephen Jacobson.

"Elric, and the Spirits of Law & Chaos" (both right). Credits: same as above.

KARL HOPF

My inspiration comes from makeup artists, cartoon animators, painters and writers. Treeman, who inhabits a peat bog, came from Norse mythology.

The face and arms were made of latex rubber, and painted with acrylic paint. Leaves and spanish moss were glued to the mask. I put black grease-paint around my eye sockets to create an illusion of depth.

"Treeman." Design, Construction & Model: Karl Hopf.

DIANE KOVALCIN

To transform ordinary fabric into a beautiful, historic gown or a terrifying monster is wonderful fun. Whether crafting intricate detail or designing something entirely out-of-this-world, no one but me knows what it is supposed to look like. But it has to look *right* and fit the story I am trying to tell on stage.

"Illegal Alien." Design, Construction & Models: Diane & Jim Kovalcin; Photo: Linda Sweeting.

70

JOHN PETERS

I have always loved H. R. Giger's designs for the movie *Alien*. But I love a good pun, too. So it wasn't too hard to invent "The Legal Alien."

This costume was built from old clothes, electric cable, telephone wire, vacuum hoses, an old seat cushion, tons of carpet foam, and four cans of gray spray paint. It was held together with a few hand stitches and dozens of safety pins. Only the beads used as eyes and the spray paint were actually purchased—a total cost of $10.00 and a mild case of chemical pneumonia.

"Legal Alien." Design, Construction & Model: John Peters; Photo: Linda Sweeting.

DENNIS MILLER

While emceeing "The Rocky Horror Picture Show," the manager told me, "Great, but get a coat." I thrift-stored one for $2. Two teenaged girls approached me on stage and gave me paint to squirt on it. That started it. I've since been adding buttons, trinkets, photos, and all sorts of dangling regalia. The used car lot flags were found in gutters after storms. With translucent capes, it has evolved into a total black-light fantasy. The costume frequently changes as old stuff wears off and new stuff is added on.

Saint "You" is extra-mortal, but has yet to achieve holiness. It is the "You" in "Happy Birthday to _____," the "I love _____" that lovers whisper in each other's ears, and the "You" personified in so many songs.

St. "You" has appeared before thousands in the Pasadena Doo-Dah Parades, as well as conventions and night clubs. A birthday cake is part of the costume.

"Saint 'You'." Design, Construction & Model: Dennis Miller; Photo: Stephen Jacobson.

PATRICIA BLACK

Akin to the age-old concept of body adornments having magical power, mine are ritual garments that transform the perception of the self. Preferring the candle-lit mysticism of other worlds, my inspiration is far removed from current fashion trends. I concentrate on rich, organic three-dimensional surface decoration, drawn from many historical and ethnic design influences outside my native Australia.

A garment is never complete for me unless it has been placed in an appropriate context. I feel my future energies will be directed toward extending the boundaries of wearable art performance or, alternatively, as sculptures placed in a natural environment would stand as monuments to celebrate my own personal mythology.

"Fossil Aeon" (left).

"Moon Goddess" (above).

"Roc" (opposite).

"Ishtar" (opposite right).

All costumes designed & constructed by Patricia Black.

"Titania & Oberon." Design, Construction & Models: Anya Martin & Phil Gilliam.

PHIL GILLIAM

I've always wanted to be an entertainer. I can go on stage in a perfectly beautiful costume, but if my presentation bombs, I'm crushed.

Another emphasis of mine is that most of the roles I play are female. This hearkens back to what masquerades were originally all about...being someone or something you're not. I think this is at the very heart of fantasy.

I often refer to myself as a "magpie" because I love "sparklies." However, I do consider myself a serious designer. Careful attention to detail can improve a simple costume and make a larger costume really shine. I don't think costume design has to come from a logical concept. Costuming is a fun and free expression.

ANYA MARTIN

As a child, costuming was a way to live out my fantasies. Putting on exotic clothes endowed the characters I invented with a reality I could feel and smell. Today I'm doing that mostly with words on paper, but every once in a while the little girl in me wants to see my characters come alive in flesh and fabric.

74

The fact that I was born on Halloween may have originally influenced my interest in costome, but by the time I was 11 years old it was much more than a once-a-year disguise. I had discovered theatre, the most fun dress-up game in the world. At 12 I discovered science fiction convention masquerades, and by 16 I was making my own costumes (up to that point my mother made all of my costumes). After high school I was ready to pursue a degree in costume design.

Why is costuming so special to me? It gives me a chance to be other people, whose lives are much more glamorous and adventurous than mine. And it's easier to meet people wearing a beautiful costume.

"The Lamentable Tale of Prince Samisen and Lady Kitsuneko." Design, Construction & Models: Fiona Leonard & Phil Gilliam; Photo: John Upton—I.N.S.

"Theatre of the Vampires." Design, Construction & Models: Anya Martin, Cynthia Holloway, Shawn Carter, Ginger Bickett, John Baker, Paul Marshall & Lonni Harvel; Photo: John Upton—I.N.S.

KATHRYN MAYER

As I am a graphic artist by profession, I regard my costuming as the ultimate product of my love for illustration.

To me, the biggest thrill is to take the original drawing and compare it to the finished costume, and see that drawing come to life. This way I can really "get inside" my artwork. The process of making a costume is the same to me as drawing or painting—I love the interplay of color, texture, line and shape. A good costume needs these same elements: light and dark values, good composition, areas of interest, areas for the eye to rest. With each new costume I also try to incorporate a new technique.

"Kelsey, the Kinetic Artist" (left). Design, Construction & Model: Kathryn Mayer; Photo: William Burnham.

"Future Evening Wear" (below). Design: Kathryn Mayer; Construction & Model: Patricia Hammer.

Drawings by Kathryn Mayer.

"Romulan Group" (opposite). Design: Kathryn Mayer; Construction & Models: Kathryn Mayer, Patricia Hammer, Patrick Sponaugle, Will Burnham & Jenne Bybel; Photo: Linda Sweeting.

"Wolf with Red Roses" (above). Design, Construction & Models: Karen & Ricky Dick; Photo: Linda Sweeting.

I didn't get to play enough "dress-up" as a child. And let's face it, there just aren't that many opportunities to play "dress-up" in adult society. People wear the ubiquitous jeans and T-shirt to holiday parties—even the opera! I enjoy working with and wearing beautiful fabrics that are not always compatible with life in the workaday world. (I love glittery fabrics, beads, and rhinestones so much that I must have been either a pack rat or a magpie in a previous life.) I often end up designing a whole outfit around an extraordinary piece of fabric or jewelry.

I have an anthropology degree and enjoy incorporating historical and ethnic design elements into my costume designs, as well as my continued interest in science fiction and fantasy, and my sense of humor. My designing roots are in the often outrageous clothes of the late '60s/early '70s, exemplified by Bob Mackie's designs for Cher and Bill Theiss' designs for "Star Trek." My costuming philosophy, in one sentence, is: I build *clothing* for alternate realities, not *costumes*.

"Coronation Gown" (opposite right). Design, Construction & Model: Karen Dick; Photo: David Bickford.

"Were-witch" (below left). Credits: Same as above.

"The Four Seasons" (below). Design, Construction & Model: Karen Dick; Photo: Chip Clark.

I tend to design *characters* rather than *costumes*. I try to think logically about what they might wear instead of making some big, glitzy thing and figuring out later what it is.

I rarely do a straight, "by-the-book" job on historicals. I prefer to use elements from history that appeal to me and interpret them into other areas. I also use more modern materials and fabrics—"They'd've used 'em if they'd've had 'em."

"Jolly Roger" (left). Design, Construction & Model: Ricky Dick; Photo: Mikey Devito.

"Leona the Leopard Lady & Hampstead Jacobs, Ringmaster" (above). Design, Construction & Models: Karen & Ricky Dick; Photo: Stephen Jacobson.

"The Amazing Puffwuzzle & Sparks the Wonder Beast" (opposite left). Design, Construction & Model: Ricky Dick; Photo: Ken Warren.

"Washtay, the White Buffalo." Design, Construction & Model: Ricky Dick; Photo: Linda Sweeting.

Costuming is a living, breathing art form that demands to be noticed. And one of the greatest things about it is: *anyone* can do it!

Sometimes I design a costume around a personality, asking myself "What would I wear if I were her?" Other times I might start with just a concept, or be inspired by a picture.

So why do I do this? There are many excuses—I mean, reasons. Being in the wrong place at the wrong time and muttering those fateful words (like so many before me), "I could do better than that!" Getting to be fascinating characters from other times, other places…other planets, without getting hauled off to the looney bin. Heavy use of controlled substances (just kidding), or tainted drinking water. Personally, it probably hasn't helped to grow up in the shadow of a nuclear power plant, or that my parents grew up there, too. Hmm, maybe it *is* in the water!

"Sacrifice" (opposite). Design, Construction & Models: Elizabeth Mayberry & friends; Photo: Linda Sweeting.

"Evil, Wicked, Mean & Nasty" (above). Design, Construction & Models: Elizabeth Mayberry, Amanda Allen, Carolyn Salemi & Denice Girardeau; Photo: Ken Warren.

"Nightmare" (right). Design, Construction & Model: Elizabeth Mayberry; Photo: Linda Sweeting.

83

PATRICIA HAMMER

I enjoy the thrill of making something beautiful out of a pile of fabric and trim. It's especially gratifying to interpret a character from literature and hear people—even the *author*—say "That's exactly what I envisioned in that story!"

"Neo Byzantine" (left). Design: Patricia Hammer & Kathryn Mayer; Construction & Model: Patricia Hammer; Photo: Will Burnham.

LAUREL CUNNINGHAM-HILL

My father is a painter and toy designer, while my mother and grandmother design and sew their own outfits. My siblings and I always had a huge box of clothes for "dress-up," and the best Halloween costumes in our neighborhood.

My "Gargoyle" has a foundation of a bodystocking, foam-core wing boards, and head bandage. The exterior is spray-painted 1/2" foam attached with hot-glue. I was able to act like stone because of the restrictiveness of the costume, much the way a king holds his regal stance in order to keep his crown on straight, or a starlet swivels her hips on stiletto heels.

I feel that when a good costumer puts on their creation, they become that character. Costuming is like having an unlimited number of personalities…and they're not all human!

This mythical "Gargoyle" comes to life to take revenge on disrespectful pigeons. Design, Construction & Model: Laurel Cunningham-Hill; Photo: Ken Warren.

SUSAN & JEFF STRINGER

I actually "feel" the beginnings of a costume welling up in my guts. Then, when the inspiration strikes, I sketch my design. Of course, the finished piece rarely ever looks exactly like my conceptual drawing.

My husband and I enjoy being other characters for awhile—not to mention the fun of watching the reactions of others watching us.

"Beauty and the Beast." Design, Construction & Models: Susan & Jeff Stringer; Photo: Libby Tucker.

"War Goblin." Design, Construction & Model: Jeff Stringer; Photo: Susan Stringer.

Costuming, for us, is a multi-dimensional art form that is a wonderful way to express ideas, feelings, and to be playful—even cathartic.

Our "Good and Evil" costumes were inspired by a "carnival" photo that made us wonder how effective a painted body stocking might be. While "Evil" required extensive padding, accessories included plaster bandages for the horns and sunglass lenses for the eyes. The most impressive effect was the deployment of our 10-foot wingspans—without the use of our arms, or elaborate hydraulics. We simply tugged our necklaces, which pulled a pin releasing our folded wings with compression springs. All of this as our staged battle of "good and evil" intensified.

"Good and Evil." Design, Construction & Models: Marian & Stephen O'Brien-Clark; Photo: Greg Bradt.

"Star Fleet Supreme Dress Uniforms." Design, Construction & Models: Marian & Stephen O'Brien-Clark; Photo: Stephen Jacobson.

Costuming is really a lot of hobbies rolled into one. For every costume project, new techniques are often learned: how to make an 18th-century corset, how to do three-dimensional foam latex makeup, how to construct sculpted breastplates…

I met my husband at a costumer's guild meeting. Our wedding was a real-life costume event. We wore Edwardian/Victorian re-creation costumes from the movie "Somewhere In Time."

"Traditional Vulcan Wedding Party." Design: Selina Harju;
Construction & Models: Selina & Mark Harju & friends;
Photo: Linda Sweeting.

"Female War Dragon." Design, Construction &
Model: Selina Harju; Photo: Linda Sweeting.

BARB SCHOFIELD

"Fire and Ice" (right). Design & Construction: Barb Schofield & Mary Hudson; Models: Barb Schofield, Mary Hudson & Martin Miller; Photo: Chip Clark.

"The Winter and Summer Queens" (below). Design & Construction: Barb Schofield; Model: Jacqueline Ward; Photos: Joe Markovic.

See page 24 for artist's statement.

"The Four Housewives of the Apocalypse" (opposite).

"Housework" (top left), by Elaine Mami.

"Gossip" (top right), by Jacqueline Ward.

"Laundry" (bottom left), by Caroline Julian.

"Cooking" (bottom right), by Barb Schofield.

Photos by John Upton—I.N.S.

SUSAN TAUBENECK & FRIENDS

"Oral Gratification" grew out of the tradition of nutritional behavior at costume conventions, consisting of the four basic food groups: salt, sugar, caffeine and alcohol. For a costumer, it's not a very large leap to decide to personify these foods. For a point of departure, each gown was based on a different historical period. The only problem we encountered was that we had more ideas than we could possibly fit on to the gowns.

"Oral Gratification." Design, Construction & Models: Susan Taubeneck, Lynn Kingsley, Marie Cooley & Judy Smith; Photo: Stephen Jacobson.

MEG HIGGINS

For many women, glamour is a natural form of play. We love the illusion, the fuss, the frill. Armor can be found in glamour. Not for the timid or faint of heart, glamour says "look at me, and look again...I'm tough, I'm smart, I'm slick." Glamour can be silly, crazy and ridiculous. That's the realm I operate in. Heap on the glitz, the fluff, the biz. I can sparkle so hard, I might make you laugh.

"I Take No Guff When I Strut My Stuff." Design & Construction: Meg Higgins; Photo: Geoffrey Carr.

SHELLY GOTTSCHAMER

As a designer, I feel privileged to create these costumes for "Peachy's Puffs," the mobile cigarette and candy girl business in San Francisco. My costumes are visible throughout the city's numerous nightclubs.

Because so many different girls wear my costumes, I make them wearable for different sizes using elastics and various lacing techniques.

The "cigarette girls" are vivacious, funny, and always attract a crowd. The "flappers" are my favorites, made to capture the style of the '20s.

"Flappers." Design & Construction: Shelly Gottschamer; Models: Eva Palomey & Camie Stepheson; Photo: Vanessa Lopez.

JULIE ZETTERBERG

While researching Chinese costumes, I became fascinated by the traditional "Empress" costume. My piece is a fantasy. The only expense was a few yards of red satin, and the narrow gold braid that outlines and defines the layers. Nearly everything else came from my junk/treasure collection.

The phoenix's wings can open and close, the head can nod, and the eyes, taken from a doll head, open and close as the head moves. My right hand, pushed through the slit midway up the jacket sleeve, controls the movement of the puppet. Hanging from my right forearm is a fake arm, made from a glove that is stuffed and wired to hold it in position. It's really a simple mechanism, but people are mystified by it.

For "The Complete Entertainer," I found a terrific buy on some mis-dyed silvery knit fabric with faint purplish blotches. It looked like alien skin. Her clothing is influenced by belly-dance outfits. The eyeballs are made from clear plastic half-balls backed with silver mylar.

"Empress of the Universe and Her Sacred Phoenix" (above). Design, Construction & Model: Julie Zeterberg; Photo: Linda Sweeting.

"The Complete Entertainer" (left) is an alien geisha, popular on many planets throughout the galaxy. Design, Construction & Model: Julie Zetterberg; Photo: Damon Hill.

DEBORAH STRUB

I've had no formal training in sewing or clothing design, but I have a Fine Arts degree in drawing and photography. Having recently discovered textile arts, I always have one or more costumes in the works. I've also become a confirmed pack rat, a condition that afflicts many costumers.

The female "Umi-Kami" has a five-layered set of kimono. The headpiece is made from 1/8" brass wire, shaped to the head, with a shell necklace and leftover pearl trim attached. The medallion in the center was made from papier-mâché, an old brooch and leftover bugle beads.

"Umi-Kami," Japanese sea-spirits embodying yin and yang, are based on Momoyama Period court garb (16th C.) Design & Construction: Deborah Strub; Models: Deborah & Bernie Strub; Photo: Thom Walls.

The winged vest of the male costume was made to resemble a coral formation. It was made of chicken wire with random intersections cut out of it, then wrapped with thin strips of papier-mâché. It was then coated with gesso, spray-painted, and dusted with glitter over a wet polymer medium. The webbed hands were made of a glisteny spandex fabric, just like gloves, but with the fabric between the fingers left intact.

"Map Dress." Design: Diane Kovalcin; Construction & Model: Julie Zetterberg; Photo: Stephen Jacobson.

93

"Coronation Ball Gown" (left) for Black Nova, rock star and Queen of England. Design & Construction: Sandy & Pierre Pettinger; Model: Sandy Pettinger; Photo: Stephen Jacobson.

Costuming allows us to express facets of our characters which are hidden or overshadowed by everyday life. Sometimes these facets are not always acceptable or appropriate in mainstream society. It can be an outlet for passions and drives which must otherwise be constrained. These exposed facets are not always "dark." Often the frivolous and child-like are as frowned upon as the grim or evil.

"Tenctonese Bride and Groom" (opposite). Design, Construction & Models: Sandy & Pierre Pettinger; Photo: John Upton—I.N.S.

"Visions of Fabergé" (below), an interpretation of Karl Fabergé's Imperial Russian Easter Eggs. Design & Construction: Sandy & Pierre Pettinger; Photo: Michael Lee Burgess.

"Ophidian King and Queen" (above). Design, Construction & Models: Sandy & Pierre Pettinger; Photo: Linda Sweeting.

DEBORAH JONES

I have always been fascinated by the limitless possibilities of what can be worn on the human body. I cannot look at anything—a piece of fabric, a bin of hardware, a sunset—without thinking about how I can use what I see, the colors and textures, in a costume. Costume is an intimate, kinetic, and democratic art form. It is art each one of us can create each day with what we have, on our own bodies, to tell ourselves and the world who we are or who we would like to be.

Some of my costumes are ordinary clothing for an imaginary culture or the future. They are usually created to solve a specific formal design problem I have set for myself, incorporating a new skill I want to learn, such as coil basketry, machine quilting, or fabric painting.

My "masquerade" costume ideas often take shape complete with music, gesture, and all aspects of performance. One theme I keep returning to is the blending of organism and machine.

Because I must travel by air to most masquerades, every piece must fold flat, or roll up, or come apart to fit in a suitcase or footlocker, and be reassembled on-site. Every costume is an adventure, climaxed by that one moment on stage when the vision comes to life.

"Counter-Culture Fashion Statement." Design drawing by Deborah Jones.

"Broken Wings." Design & Model: Deborah Jones; Construction: Deborah & Terry Jones; Photo: Linda Sweeting. Detail of back (left) shows blinking lights. Photo: Janet Moe.

"Ceremonial Garb for Female Shaman."
Design: Deborah Jones; Construction &
Model: Carolyn Kayta Martz; Photos:
Stephen Jacobson. (Details of Head &
Back also shown.)

ELEANOR FARRELL

My fascination with costume stems from its synthetic nature. I like to combine elements from different sources, try out new techniques and play with images and effects. I enjoy visual puns: "Red Sonja Henje", a pearl-handled Colt with real pearls, a "Socket Wench."

For me, costuming is preferably a social endeavor, and I have found that costumers in general are very generous and enthusiastic playmates. I enjoy making things that other people have designed as much as designing my own pieces. In collaborating with other costumers, particularly on performance pieces, the different perspectives and skills each person contributes makes the project a learning experience as well as a very exciting creative process.

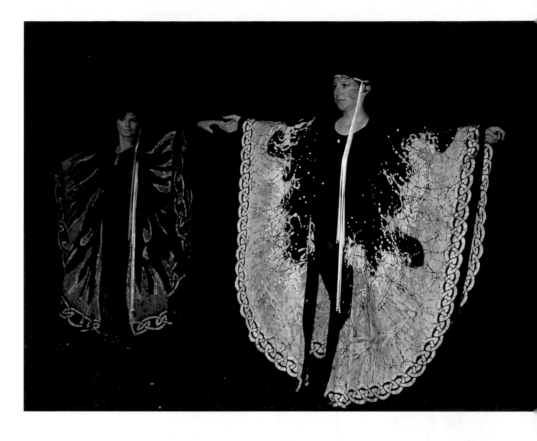

"Ghosts in the Machine" (opposite). Robots fashion their own ghost costumes, with South Pacific influence. Eleanor Farrell & Deborah Jones; Photo: Stephen Jacobson.

"Airs of Sea & Fire" (above). Design, Construction & Models: Eleanor Farrell & Deborah Jones.

"Alliance" (below), between two hostile tribes of fairies. Eleanor Farrell & Deborah Jones; Photos: John Willis.

I love costuming and I hate costuming, but I need to costume—isn't that a sort of definition of an obsession? For me, the "love" part is that I get to wear something wonderfully unique, and hopefully cause a stir of excitement. The "hate" part is that I have to labor over every detail of a costume's construction. When asked why I costume, I say "I don't believe in wasting time, money or effort on minor vices."

Like most creative acts, costuming is probably 1% inspiration and 99% perspiration. After the concept comes analysis, research, discovery, failure, success, frustration, elation; and as I near completion: a panicked frenzy, extreme excitement (and irritability), and finally, after the presentation, a happy, relieved exhaustion—yes, I know, it's a lot like sex.

"Lady from a Pleasure Planet" (above). Design, Construction & Model: Angelique Trouvere.

"Futuristic Barbarienne" (right). Design, Construction & Model: Angelique Trouvere; Photo: Chip Clark.

I enjoy creating both original and re-creation costumes. I feel that re-creations have an undeserved reputation as a sort of step-child of costuming. It is very demanding and exacting work — 110% perspiration — requiring every line, seam, and stitch to be perfect. Original design, on the other side of the sequin, can be wonderfully refreshing. And after all, inspiration is all around us!

"Daggit" (left), from "Battlestar: Galactia." Design, Construction & Model: Angelique Trouvere; Photo: Mark Witz.

"The Lilac Fairy" (above). Design, Construction & Model: Angelique Trouvere; Photo: Kristopher Curling, courtesy of Doctors in the House.

I've always been interested in "Fancy Dress," as they call it in England. As a child, I copied costumes in the Ice Capades for my "Miss Revlon doll." I always dressed up for Halloween, and when I outgrew that, I chaperoned younger children around the neighborhood, wearing my older sister's prom dress.

"King and Queen of Cups" (below). Design, Construction & Models: Kathy & Drew Sanders; Photo: Sandy Cohen.

"Queen of Wands" (above). Design, Construction & Model: Kathy Sanders; Photo: Chip Clark.

Being a fan of "Star Trek" led me to Science Fiction conventions in the late '60s. Here was an environment where dressing up, in the "Masquerade," was accepted and even encouraged. I enjoy designing, but even more, I enjoy the process involved in figuring out how to make it. Sewing isn't the only technique used. Hot glue, feather work, foam sculpture, beading: there are many techniques to be learned.

One of my major regrets is not having the kind of budget for my own work that some of the companies I've worked for have had for their projects. From Tarot cards, to cartoon characters, from kings and queens to raisins and peaches, costuming has become a part of my life.

"Bridal Gown" (above). Design, Construction & Model: Kathy Sanders; Photo: Stephen Jacobson.

"Wedding Attire" (right). Design, Construction & Models: Kathy & Drew Sanders; Photo: Linda Sweeting.

"The Rape of the Lock" (opposite). Design, Construction & Models: Kathy & Drew Sanders; Photo: Chip Clark.

"Mombi & the Wheeler" (below). Design, Construction & Models: Kathy & Drew Sanders; Photo: Ken Warren.

"The Handmaiden of Death and her Groom" (above). Design, Construction & Models: Kathy & Drew Sanders; Photo: John Upton—I.N.S.

As a child, the "dress-up box" always lived in my closet. I may have grown up, but I've never grown out of the sheer fun of dressing up—and my closet is still full of costumes.

I enjoy the texture, the weight, drape, color and "feel" of the materials I work with; how they feel to handle, to wear, to look at. All of my costumes are made to be worn—to be "experienced." Primarily I work for myself, but it also gives me great pleasure to see someone else enjoying the work of my hands and the imagery in my head.

It is a creative shaping of thought into form in some sort of meaningful fashion—but mostly, it's fun.

"In the Court of Havnor" (right). Design, Construction & Model: Jennifer Tifft; Photo: Stephen Jacobson.

"The Musketeer from Mars" (opposite). Design, Construction & Model: Jennifer Tifft; Photo: Michael Jhon.

"Daughter of Fishes." Design, Construction & Model: Jennifer Tifft; Photo: Linda Sweeting.

KEVIN ROCHE

Costuming is a way to reach out: to express an idea in such a way as to capture someone's imagination and let them share the fantasy, the joke, or the vision—if only for a moment.

I like to remind people (and myself) that the world is *not* a dull, mundane place, but is always filled with the possibility of excitement and magic—if only we take a moment to look.

"Aurahi—Water" (left) & "Helion—Fire" (below). Design, Construction & Models: Kevin Roche & Jennifer Tifft; Photos: Michael Jhon.

"Court Robe of Kesse" (left). Design: Jennifer Tifft;
Construction & Model: Kevin Roche; Photo: David
Bickford.

"Princess Takiyashi" (above), demon princess from
a Kabuki opera. Design, Construction & Model: Kevin
Roche; Photo: Chip Clark.

Cynthia Fena

Since I've been a dental hygienist for the past twenty years, wearing a belly dance costume allows me to show my more sensual, creative, feminine side.

I try to thematically demonstrate in the costume some of the elements of the dance I plan to perform when I wear it. This helps me express myself more convincingly.

I can't help but think that my patients might respond better if this costume was my uniform.

JULIE NICKELL

I am a professional belly dancer. I really love the dance. I express myself through my moves and my costumes. When I put my costume on, I transform my whole being into the dance, and seem to acquire the power to have an audience under my spell.

The beauty of this costume is combining the topaz stones and gold bugle-beads to bring out the creamy color of the pearls. In my field, I am known as the dancer who makes costumes for the dancer.

"Julia"

Everyone has infinite possibilities, but most never realize them. As illusionists, costumers make words into cloth, drawings into flesh, imagination into reality. Everything I wear is costume: painter's jumpsuits, PT-A jacket dresses, the Queen of Air and Darkness...Who would suspect all these disparate characters actually are me? And yet, nothing I do feels foreign to me; all come from something in my subconscious that says: "You must be this."

Knowing that, I know the hearts of other women costumers; they are goddesses, priestesses and queens. The variety and richness of the world of costuming delights me. Reading science fiction all my life has rewarded me with entry into that world.

> "...that which we are, we are;
>   One equal temper of heroic hearts."
>   —Tennyson

"The Sundancer" (below). Design & Construction: Marjii Ellers; Model: Ernst Ellersieck; Photo: Stephen Jacobson.

"The Black Queen" (right). Design, Construction & Model: Marji Ellers; Photo: Walt Daughtery.

When I first discovered costuming 12 years ago, I recognized it as a chance to put an overactive imagination to good use. I wasn't any good at drawing or writing, but I knew the basics of sewing and set out to teach myself the fundamentals of beads, sequins, appliqué and all manner of shiny fabric. Since then, it has

"Spirit of the Greenwood."
Design, Construction & Model: Jacqueline Ward;
Photo: John Upton—I.N.S.

become an opportunity to create three-dimensional wearable art and, in its presentation, an escape from an otherwise mundane existence.

Initially I combed through books for inspiration, looking for characters to portray in costume. Looking into their personalities and behaviors provided numerous clues for costume ideas. Most recently, my "Dreamweaver" and "Spirit of the Greenwood" costumes evolved from interpretations of concepts rather than characters.

Despite the discomforts of a heavy costume, makeup and headdress, I find it fairly easy to slip into character. What makes it all worthwhile is the tremendous thrill of hearing the audience respond, and knowing that they appreciate and hopefully understand what I have tried to convey through fabric, hardware and decoration.

"Lady Epone" (above) from "The Many Colored Land." Design, Construction & Model: Jacqueline Ward; Photo: Chip Clark.

"The Goddess Glitziana," with Devotee (right). Design & Construction: Jacqueline Ward; Models: Jacqueline Ward & Kathryn Condon; Photo: David Bickford.

"Wicked Fairy Carabosse" (right) from "The Sleeping Beauty." Design, Construction & Model: Jacqueline Ward; Photo: Paul Jeremias.

114

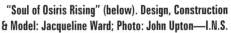

"Dreamweaver" (opposite top) shows shifting aspects of sleep and dream cycles. Design, Construction & Model: Jacqueline Ward; Photos: Stephen Jacobson.

"Soul of Osiris Rising" (below). Design, Construction & Model: Jacqueline Ward; Photo: John Upton—I.N.S.

"Cinderella 3000" (above), whose glass slipper has evolved into an entire gown of glass. Design, Construction & Model: Jacqueline Ward; Photo: John Upton—I.N.S.

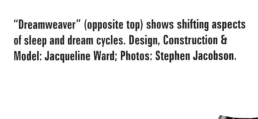

Using the painterly manipulation of materials and texture, made from wood, silk, paper, gold leaf enamel and ceramics, I approach theatre and dance through the medium of sculpture. I hope my work moves people to a path where movement and stillness meet, and where, intertwined with a labyrinth of delicate props, shreds of memory lace into an ephemeral drama of a thousand intricate pieces, slowly moving, stirring us toward a sense of patience and timelessness.

All is changing, passing through us, against us, and moving away again. This is the drama that moves each of us so profoundly. It is only that moment of consciousness that makes it appear as though it were done with deliberation—when it was actually just perfect chaos that happened to look good. Out of complexity comes a whole.

My work is intended to inspire people to remember their mythical pasts and primal roots in Nature—all connected to each other by a network of tiny spinning gems, that we all will disappear back into our Earth, to begin again.

"The Tin Twin" (below) in one phase of performance. Design, Construction & Model: Sha Sha Higby; Photo: Albert Hollander.

"Pineapple Sunset" (opposite) was made by the artist in India from the ikat silk of Orissa. This performance costume is also composed of thousands of pounded silken tussah feathers stitched by eight Indian tailors, and painted by the miniaturists of Jaipur. The inset photo shows the main body of the costume. Design, Construction & Model: Sha Sha Higby; Photo: Albert Hollander.

"Fuka" (right) was the artist's first performance piece. Design, Construction & Model: Sha Sha Higby.

"A Bee on the Beach" (below). Snake skins rattle in the sand for a dance of forty wriggling fingers, fans and flags. Design, Construction & Model: Sha Sha Higby; Photo: Albert Hollander.

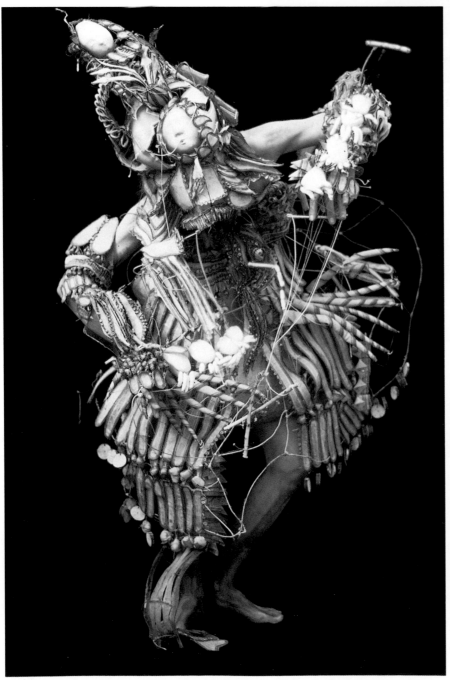

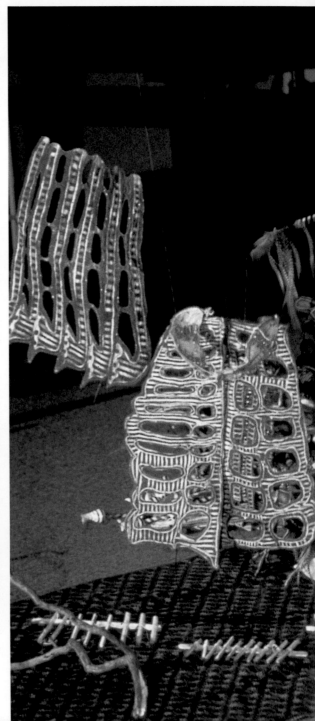

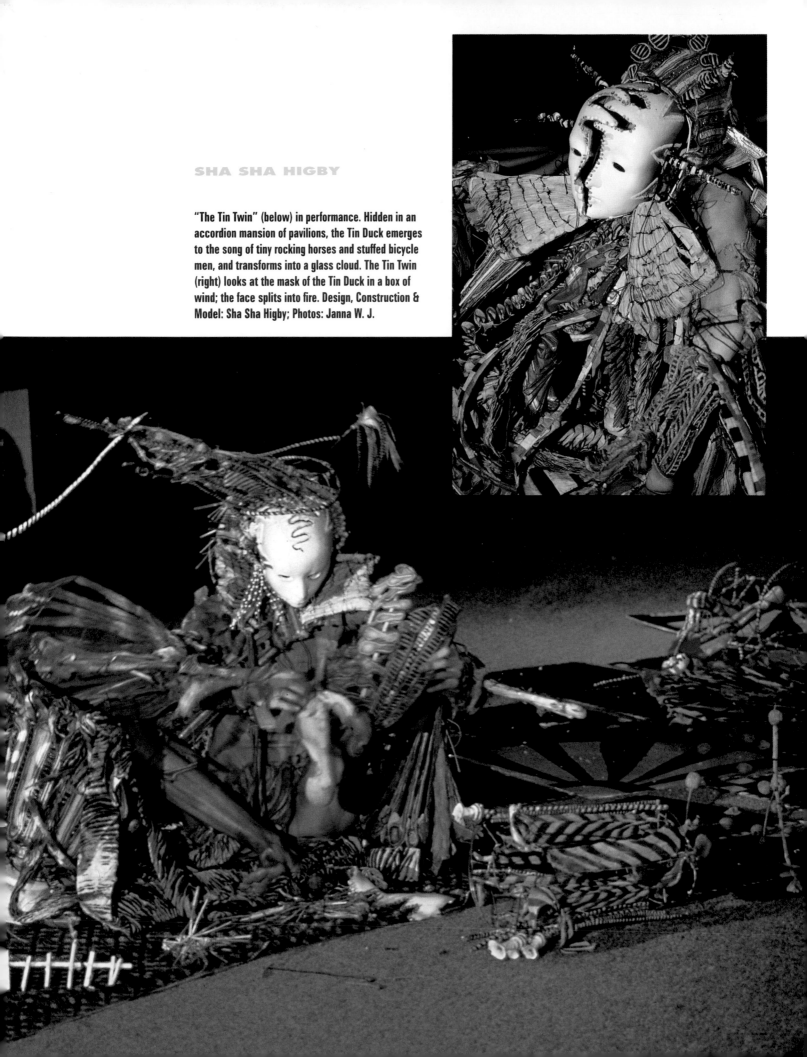

SHA SHA HIGBY

"The Tin Twin" (below) in performance. Hidden in an accordion mansion of pavilions, the Tin Duck emerges to the song of tiny rocking horses and stuffed bicycle men, and transforms into a glass cloud. The Tin Twin (right) looks at the mask of the Tin Duck in a box of wind; the face splits into fire. Design, Construction & Model: Sha Sha Higby; Photos: Janna W. J.

"Cows Under a Pepper Tree" (opposite). The cycles of birth, death and rebirth are enacted in a tiny town of wooden gates, flaming houses, mechanical birds, spindles and mirrors. Design, Construction & Model: Sha Sha Higby; Photo: Fred Mertz.

"Moon Puppets" (below) outdoor performance begins in a black robe, then breaks into a whimsical lacey costume, surrounded by small chairs which are knocked over in a dance with spiraled sticks. Top photo shows detail of puppet. Design, Construction & Model: Sha Sha Higby; Photos: Ilka Hartmann.

FUTURISTIC

ESTELLE AKAMINE

Perhaps Adam and Eve's fall from grace had the greatest impact upon my creativity. I work close to the body. Clothing is an image that never fails to excite me or arouse my curiosity. Within the concept of body coverings is a complete universe of potential forms.

Concepts of cloth and clothing emerged as the structure of my work, but the human psyche became the subject matter. The cloth layer seemed to easily represent the ritualistic self, while inside, with an implied or actual body, the ecstatic, duped, or angered true self is revealed.

My design rule is this: Forget you are making clothing. Pretend you are cooking food or building an addition to your house. Remembering sewing rules will only inhibit the process in predictable ways. I say that I build my work, and, indeed, the look is somewhat architectural. I like this kind of ambiguity: otherwise, clothing can be such a serious, tedious business.

The idea for my wearable art comes from wanting to make art out of nothing, or art out of recyclable materials. My credo is: "If you can lift it, you can wear it."

Alien character from "Cabaret of the 21st Century" (opposite). Design & Construction: Estelle Akamine; Photo: Judy Reed.

"Nymph Dress" (above). Design & Construction: Estelle Akamine.

A scene from the Footloose Dance Theater Company's "Akamine Bound," a parody of ramp fashion shows (right). Design & Construction: Estelle Akamine.

"Trio" (below). Design & Construction: Estelle Akamine; Photo: Sandy Clifford.

"Cocktail Dress." Design & Construction:
Estelle Akamine.

Gladiator & Android from "Cabaret of the 21st Century." Design &
Construction: Estelle Akamine; Photo: Kenneth Chen.

125

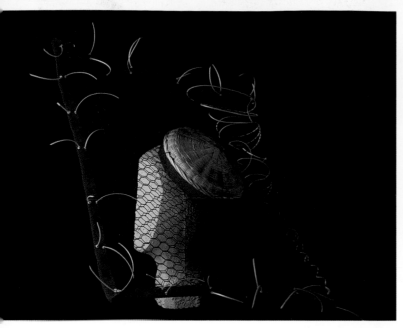

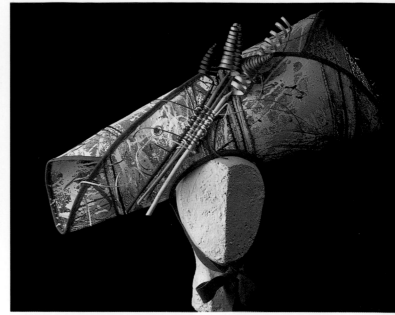

ESTELLE AKAMINE

"Chinese Chicken Hat" (top left) & "Carnival Hat" (top right). Design & Construction: Estelle Akamine; Photos: Joshua Ets-Hokins.

"Fur Collared Jacket." Design & Construction: Estelle Akamine; Photo: Fred White.

JANUWA MOJA

The act of creating is a ritual for me. My idea is to take the canvas off the easel and wear it. The wearer becomes the art piece.

In my last twenty years as a designer, I have found inspiration in my travels to Africa, Brazil, London and Paris. My major influence is African, but I draw on a variety of cultures. I often create my own fabrics, incorporating raw materials such as crushed metals.

Many of my garments result from consultations with clients: getting a feel for their personality, the intent of the garment, and the occasion for which it will be worn. My creations may even contribute a certain "shock value" to the trendiest of this city's evening events. Washington is like a big playground for me.

"Fulavi Princess" (above) features handmade paper head-piece and collar. Design, Construction & Model: Januwa Moja; Photo: Richard Green.

"Mystery History" (left) features Foluke Bady modelling "Egyptian Sunset" and Januwa Moja modelling "Return of the Phoenix." Design & Construction: Januwa Moja; Photo: Richard Green.

TERRY NIEDZIALEK

Hair Montage crosses the boundaries between plastic art, performance art, and fashion. It was invented out of a vision of hair used as a sculptural material, and expresses social and political statements about the relationship between man, nature, and technology. I see the head as a miniature earth waiting to be personified, given the earth's energies through the particular environment into which the hair is built. This expresses the oneness of people and their environment—we become the living energy of it.

Primitive cultures used to adorn their hair with twigs and other materials as a part of their ritual, spiritual life. My creations are more than a redefinition of beauty. They are intended to transform our level of consciousness about our own relationship to our environment.

128

"America the Beautiful" (opposite left). Design & Construction: Terry Niedzialek; Photo: Julius Vitali.

"The Bride's Lighthouse" (opposite right). Credits: same as above.

"The Green House Effect" (left). Design & Construction: Terry Niedzialek; Photo: Julius Vitali.

"Live TV" (below left). Credits: same as above.

"Industrial Hair Sculpture" (below right). Credits: same as above.

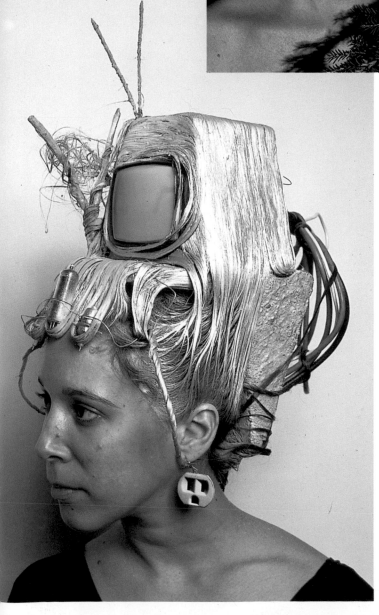

CHRISTEN BROWN & CAROL MCKIE MANNING

Our work endeavors to capture a sense of the mythical and the magical, and to stitch it down onto fabric which is then transformed into a kind of ritual costume. We imagine that the person wearing the garment will be empowered simply by wearing the piece.

When we collaborate on a costume we begin by getting together to discuss ideas, fabrics, and a general direction for the work. The actual construction involves hundreds of hours as the piece travels back and forth between our studios. We consciously avoid limiting each other's artistic contributions so that the work is in a constant state of metamorphosis. It's always been surprising and exciting to see where the other has gone with an idea. From this creative process, we have learned new techniques from each other. Our most recent work has included painted, appliquéd, and embroidered signs and symbols that are meant to evoke ancient cultural memories or to conjure fantasy worlds.

"When the Medicine Woman Weaves her Spell, the Snake Charmer Begins to Dance" (opposite left). Design & Construction: Carol McKie Manning & Christen Brown; Model: Jean Olson; Photo: Tom Henderson.

"Celestial Symphony of the Summer Solstice" (opposite right). Design & Construction: Christen Brown & Carol McKie Manning; Photo: Fairfield Processing Corp.

"The Chrystal Maiden from the Isle of Fire and Ice" (right). Design & Construction: Christen Brown & Carol McKie Manning; Photo: Tom Henderson.

SUSAN NININGER

My work with costume as an art form began in 1972, as a student in ceramics, and continues today with my work as a costume designer in the film industry. My art costumes, or costume sculpture, are those pieces that allow me to express my thoughts and feelings visually in the creation of a costume image. They are created as a device for imaginative stimulation, not only for the viewer, but also for those who might wear them. It is most fulfilling for me as a costume artist to give my costumes to performers so that they may then give the costume another breath of life with their movement images. This collaboration is, for me, part of the magic of costume as an art form: that it lives and grows even after my hands have "finished" with it.

Costumes for "King" (opposite), a commercial for United Airlines. Design & Construction: Susan Nininger; Model (top): Tia; Photos: Elissa Zimmerman.

Marianna Tcherkassky (right), from The American Ballet Theatre, and David Palmer (below) performing in the film "To Dream of Roses," a project for the Sumitomo Pavilion 1990 Expo, Osaka, Japan. Design & Construction: Susan Nininger; Photos: Ann Marsden.

"Royal Warrior" (opposite). Design & Construction: Susan Nininger; Model: John Nash Abdul; Photo: Lawrence Manning.

"Hopi Kachina" (left). Design & Construction: Susan Nininger; Model: choreographer/dancer Louise Salisbury; Photo: Jim Cummins.

"Going: Fishing" (right). Design & Construction: Susan Nininger; Model: Ruth Pelz; Photo: Roger Schrieber.

134

ZEPHRA MAY MILLER

Inspiration came for this work when I ran out of yarn while trying to finish one of my Chic Designs for a showing. The plastic garbage bags were handy, and have proven to be quite comfortable to wear. The open "chain link" allows for ventilation in summer, and the denser "close crochet" provides warmth in winter. You forget it's plastic as it becomes a second skin, which stretches with body heat to fit any form.

My garbage bags are but a shadow of mankind, transformed into beautiful, functional conversation pieces. Someday I'd like to wear my Chic Designs in Paris and meet Sonia Rykiel, queen of fashion.

"Stringing You Along..." (above). Design & Construction: Zephra May Miller; Photo: Geoffrey Carr.

"Channel 15" (left). Design & Construction: Zephra May Miller; Photo: Geoffrey Carr.

RENEE SHERRER

I am interested in taking materials which have had a previous "life" and using them in such a way as to resurrect aspects of that life, creating new ways in which they can be regarded.

I like to make art which expresses the human condition. My tendency is to make work which moves with your body, defines or exaggerates the human shape, and expresses or allows experimentation with your personality.

My basic motivation is to find a way to combine the ridiculous and sublime, where the craftsmanship reflects the quality of the idea...and to have a good time doing it!

"Brassiere Prom Dress 2" (left). Design, Construction & Photo: Renee Sherrer.

"Pasta Dress" (bottom right). Credits: same as above.

"Glove Boa" (below left). Design & Construction: Renee Sherrer; Photo: Frank Ferguson.

MARILYN ANNIN

Through the centuries women have found pleasure in reworking leftover bits and pieces into something special for others to enjoy—whether it's making quilts, casseroles or, in my case, sculptured garments.

My path to these garments began in my work as a painter, and a friend's suggestion that I help teach a sculpture class. The class focused on teaching painters to think in three-dimensional terms. Rather than taking a more formal approach to sculpture using marble, bronze or wood, I decided to experiment with materials that I handled daily: buttons, safety pins, zippers, neckties, costume jewelry, and other discarded or forgotten objects.

The next step came after several months of working with these gathered objects, when a fellow artist picked up a half-finished piece and threw it over her shoulders. As this scrap of art conformed to her figure, I saw the wide-ranging possibilities of a new-found medium.

At that recognition, my involvement in the sculptures expanded from the technical aspect of making art into working with ideas: a series of sculptured garments, each acting as a metaphor for a specific attitude or custom of our culture.

"The Gift" (above). Design & Construction: Marilyn Annin.

"Shawl" (right). Credits: same as above.

"His Precious Jewel" (opposite). Design & Construction: Marilyn Annin.

138

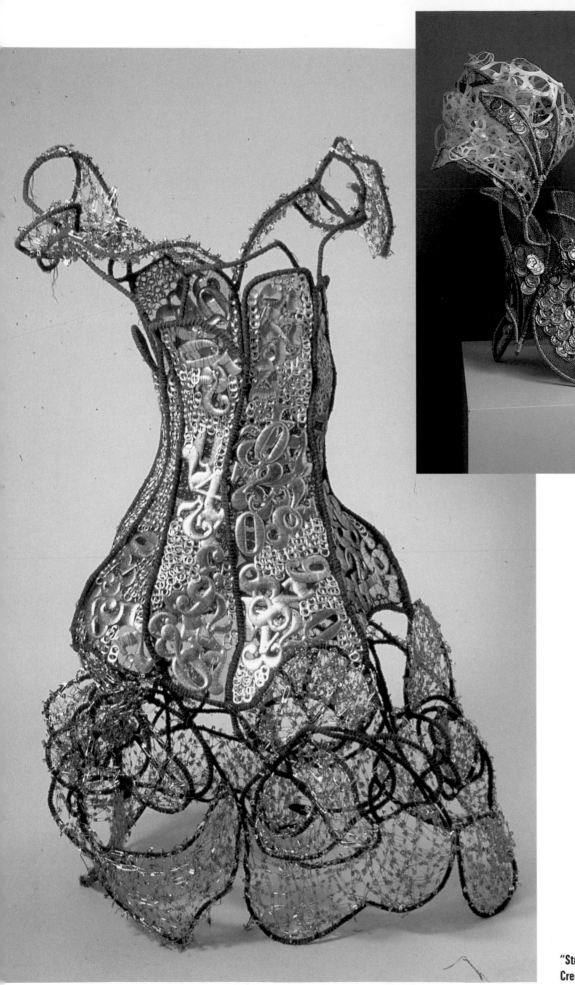

Costume for the dance "Nutcracker" (above).
Design & Construction: Marilyn Annin.

"Striving for Perfection" (left).
Credits: same as above.

Costume for the dance "West Side Story" (above). Design & Construction: Marilyn Annin.

"King of the Mountain" (right). Credits: same as above.

JUNG HAE KIM

Most of the inspiration for my costumes comes from listening to music. Some of my works are called "paper costumes," but these are woven and sculpted from various wires—copper, brass, and aluminum. The organic relationship between clothing and human movement provides the basis for this formative art, which is a metaphor of myself. It is said that my works are "sophisticated, feminine expressions...containing a deep sensitivity to materials, and infused with Oriental shamanism."

"The Living Water" (above).
Design & Construction:
Jung Hae Kim.

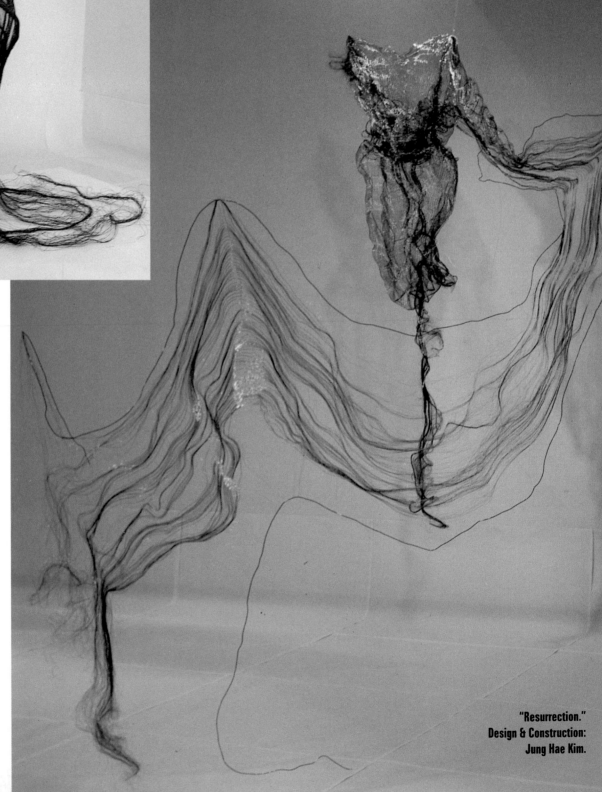

"Resurrection."
Design & Construction:
Jung Hae Kim.

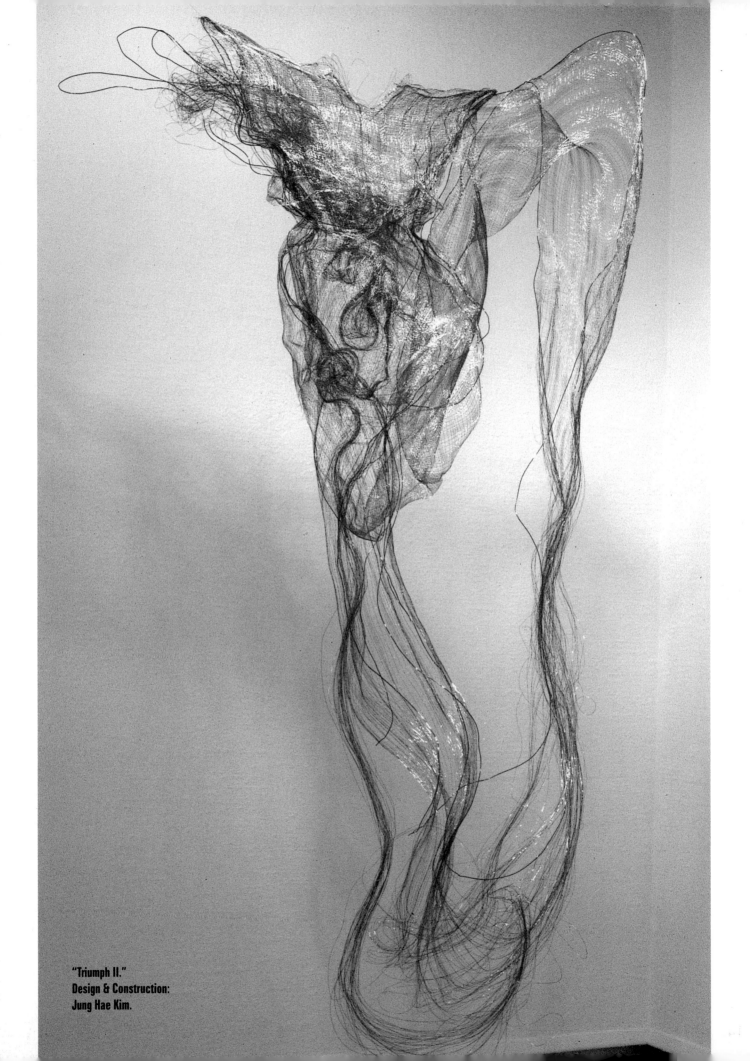

"Triumph II."
Design & Construction:
Jung Hae Kim.

INTERNATIONAL COSTUMERS' GUILDS

Greater Columbia Fantasy Costumers' Guild
P.O. Box 683
Columbia, MD 21045

Costumers' Guild West
c/o Janet Anderson
3216 Villa Knolls Dr.
Pasadena, CA 91107

The Great White North Costumers' Guild
c/o Costumers' Workshop
Box 784 Adelaide St. PO
Toronto, Ontario, CANADA M5C 2K1

The NY/NJ Costumers' Guild
(aka The Sick Pups of Monmouth County)
c/o Mami
85 West McClellan Ave.
Livingston, NJ 07039

Midwest Costumers' Guild
c/o Pettinger
2709 Everett
Lincoln, NE 68502

Wild and Woolly Costumers' Guild
PO Box 1088 Station M
Calgary, Alberta, CANADA T2P 2K9

Rocky Mountain Costumers' Guild
3522 Smuggler Way
Boulder, CO 80303-7222

Deep South Costumers' Guild
c/o D. L. Burden
1649 28th Ave. S.
Homewood, AL 35209

New England Costumers' Guild
(aka The Boston Tea Party and Sewing Circle)
c/o Carter
120 Eames St.
Wilmington, MA 01887

Confederate Costumers' Guild
c/o Susan Stringer
3947 Atlanta Dr.
Chattanooga, TN 37416

Lunatic Fringe Costumers' Guild
c/o Vicki Warren
1139 Woodmere Road
Pottstown, PA 19464

PYMWYA Costumers' Guild
(People Your Mother Warned You About)
c/o Animal X
7201 Meade St.
Pittsburgh, PA 15208

Montreal Costumers' Guild
2274A Beaconsfield Ave.
Montreal, Quebec, CANADA H4A 2G8

Southwest Costumers' Guild
c/o Patti Cook
3820 W. Flynn
Phoenix, AZ 85019

INDEX

A
Akamine, Estelle.............................12, 122
Allen, Kenneth...23
Anderson, Janet Wilson................8, 21, 62
Annin, Marilyn..138

B
Black, Patricia..72
Bradbury, Rae...61
Brown, Christen..........................2, 3, 130
Butterfield, Adrian..............................18, 68

C
Cunningham-Hill, Laurel............................84

D
DeWinter, Jwlhyfer...................................28
Dick, Karen & Ricky.............................78, 80

E
Ellers, Marjii......................................9, 111

F
Farrrell, Eleanor.......................................98
Fena, Cynthia...110
Fink, Sally..53

G
Gilliam, Phil..74
Girardeau, Denice.....................................52
Gottschamer, Shelly..................................91

H
Hammer, Patricia......................................84
Harju, Selina & Mark.................................87
Higby, Sha Sha.......................4, 13, 116
Higgins, Meg..90
Historical Reenactment.............................37
Holloman, Jeannette.................................36
Hopf, Karl...70
Hoyt-Heydon, Mela & Friends....................41
Hyll, Julia Ann..46

J
Jones, Deborah....................10, 96, 98

K
Keeler, Jana..32
Ketcham, Jennifer................................36, 67
Kim, Jung Hae...142
Kovalcin, Diane...................................70, 93
Kuykendall, Karen.....................................54

L
Leonard, Fiona..75
Lewis, Robin...50

M
MacDermott, Dana & Bruce.......................56
Manning, Carol McKie...............2, 3, 130
Martin, Anya...74
Mayberry, Elizabeth & Friends...................82
Mayer, Kathryn...76
Miller, Dennis...71
Miller, Zephra May...................................136
Moja, Januwa..127
Moore, Cherie...33

N
Nickell, Julie..110
Niedzialek, Terry......................................128
Nininger, Susan...............................6, 132

O
O'Brien-Clark, Marian & Stephen..............86
Off the Wall..58
Ontis, Elizabeth Pidgeon & Carl..........11, 38

P
Peters, John..71
Pettinger, Sandy & Pierre..........................94

R
Rickard, Patricia..31
Ridenour, Victoria..............7, 15, 18, 68
Roche, Kevin...108
Ross, Wendy.....................................17, 64

S
Salemi, Carolyn..................................40, 60
Sanders, Kathy & Drew............................102
Schofield, Barb...................................24, 88
Sherrer, Renee..137
Smith-Gharet, Lita.....................................22
Soft Touch, The...26
Stringer, Susan & Jeff................................85
Strub, Deborah...93

T
Taubeneck, Susan & Friends......................90
Tifft, Jennifer.....................................36, 106
Trimmer, Jeannie.......................................41
Trouvere, Angelique..........................35, 100
Tucker, Lani..30

V
Vandervort, Vandy.....................................48

W
Ward, Jacqueline......................................112

X
X, Animal............................16, 34, 42

Z
Zetterberg, Julie.......................................92